THE AUTHENTIC
TAROT

Thomas Saunders has been a professional Tarot reader for the past 18 years and has taught many seminars in the UK and America. He was a regular broadcaster on the subject on the Pete Murray Show for LBC London Radio and in 1993 became the Tarot expert for *Marie Claire* magazine for three years.

He is a practising dowser and long-time member of The National Federation of Spiritual Healers. He is an Associate Lecturer at the University of the Arts, London, and has delivered lectures at the Royal Academy for the British Society of Dowsers, The Prince's Foundation, The Research Into Lost Knowledge Organisation (RILKO), Kairos and other groups covering the decoding of myths and fairy tales, mystery school teachings and sacred geometry.

See www.thomassaunders.net for further information.

THE AUTHENTIC
TAROT

Discovering Your Inner Self

THOMAS SAUNDERS

WATKINS PUBLISHING
LONDON

This edition published in the UK 2007
by Watkins Publishing, Sixth Floor, Castle House,
75–76 Wells Street, London W1T 3QH

1 3 5 7 9 10 8 6 4 2

Designed and typeset by Jerry Goldie

Printed and bound in Great Britain

British Library Cataloguing-in-Publication data available

ISBN 978-1-905857-15-9

www.watkinspublishing.com

'*The Authentic Tarot* is a wise combination of classical wisdom, the dynamics of myths and psychological interpretations of the profound symbolic language that is the Tarot.'

A T Mann, author of *The Mandala Astrological Tarot* and *Secrets of the Tarot*.

'What a wonderful, inspiring and unique book!

Thomas Saunders has managed to capture the very essence of Tarot and its real profound meaning. With pristine clarity and deep understanding of the subject he guides the reader through the maze of complicated and intricate symbols which represent various stages in an individual's development on their way to self-knowledge, the knowledge of the inner Self.

Thomas Saunders makes it clear from the start in his book that we are not to be presented with a 'manual' on fortune-telling but with a very special, highly spiritually-charged guided tour to the core of our inner Self. He makes us realise why we are here on this very beautiful planet, what is the purpose of our life's journey, and what we tend to forget in the mad rush of our every day life.

Anybody who is interested in the deep knowledge of the Tarot will find this book enlightening. Do not miss the chance to read this book, it is a real jewel.'

Dr Jill Claxton-Oldfield

'A landmark work of great significance! With ease and grace, Thomas brings to life the hidden truths of some of the world's greatest mysteries regarding the human psyche.'

Dr Norma Milanovich, Author of *The Light Shall Set You Free, We, The Arcturians*, and *Sacred Journey to Atlantis*.

'Thomas Saunders gives a fascinating and unique insight to the Tarot. The book offers the reader great hope and inspiration in that by the correct use of the Tarot a person can take responsibility for their own life and control their destiny. Truly an eye opener!'

Sarika Jobanputra
Director, S J Associates Ltd, Chartered Certified Accountants

'Not only a thorough and in-depth guide to the meaning and symbolism of the Tarot, this book contains powerful lessons for living a better life. It skilfully guides the reader to use the Tarot in the way in which they were first intended. Thomas remains objective whilst respecting those who have contributed to the craft since its inception.

A beautiful and concise history of the Tarot is woven effortlessly into the fabric of the book and takes the reader on a journey which examines the archetypes, metaphors and symbolism with which we are all innately familiar. Thomas creates a space for the reader to examine their personal journey through the story of the Tarot and invites us to accept responsibility for where we are in our lives and draw on our own inner strength

Whether an experienced Tarot reader or a beginner, this book offers a wealth of knowledge, and the opportunity to explore the meaning and symbolism of the Tarot on a level the likes of which I am yet to encounter in a single work. A must-read for all who want to deepen their knowledge and experience in this area.'

Marilyn Devonish
Director, Trance Formations

Prefatory note about the
Ancien Tarot de Marseille

The BP Grimaud edition of the *Ancien Tarot de Marseille* featured in this book is the recommended version as the reproduction of the images is of the highest quality and the best clarity of colour. The deck is published in both French and English by France Cartes.

To my dear grandson Leon

CONTENTS

ACKNOWLEDGEMENTS

It is unlikely that this book would have been written without the loving encouragement, help and support of my wife Janet.

I am also indebted to John Baldock for his editorial skills, knowledge, advice and for kindly writing a most erudite Foreword to the book.

My thanks go to the anonymous David and Zoe for allowing me to publish their Tarot readings.

A very special thanks and acknowledgement to France Cartes for their kind permission to reproduce the images of the BP Grimaud edition of the *Ancien Tarot de Marseille*.

I also extend my thanks to all those who have granted me permission to publish extracts of the quotations.

FIGURES WITHIN TEXT

COLOUR PLATES

FOREWORD

We all have in us a book to write, or so the saying goes, and we naturally assume this to mean that we have a novel or a book of poetry lying dormant within us, waiting until such time as we put pen to paper or fingers to computer keyboard. 'One day,' we say, 'I really must sit down and write my book. One day ...' Yet in reality we are already writing our book. It is the book of our life, and we are writing it every day. In fact, we have been writing it ever since we came into this world; but we rarely stop to read what we have written. By this I don't mean replaying our memories of the people, the events and the places that have featured in our lives up until now. These are merely the words in our book, so to speak. Like words, they have meaning. But for these disparate elements to have meaning we need to string them together, like words on a page, into sentences and paragraphs until they form a coherent story. Even then, the deeper meaning of our own personal story will probably still escape us, for when it comes to reading the book of our life we are faced with a problem: we have never been taught how to read what we are writing.

This perhaps explains why we rarely look beyond the superficialities of life – the 'words' on the pages of our book – for something deeper and more fulfilling that will enhance both the meaning and purpose of our lives. And yet such instruction has always been available, although it is often dismissed as belonging to the realm of the 'occult'. Nowadays, the word 'occult' is widely interpreted as meaning 'supernatural', and is often used to infer that something is 'dark' or 'evil'. But in its original sense – and in the sense in which Thomas Saunders uses it throughout this book – it simply means 'hidden' (from the Latin *occulo*, 'to hide'). Whilst occult knowledge is sometimes deliberately hidden in order to prevent its abuse or debasement, it frequently remains hidden because it lies beyond our current level of understanding. Hence the reason for the existence of the world's many initiatic traditions: their function is to initiate the individual, step by step, into ever deeper levels of understanding of themselves and their place within the overall scheme of things. These initiatic traditions are also sometimes referred to as 'mystery' or 'mystical' traditions because of the revealing insights they offer their initiates into what, up until the moment of initiation or revelation, has been a mystery beyond the realms of their understanding. The Tarot is one such initiatic or mystery tradition. But as Thomas Saunders reveals, it is also more than this: it is a book that holds the keys to understanding the 'book of life' that we ourselves are writing.

Just like the words in a printed book, the people, events and places that feature in our book of life are instantly recognizable for what they are: people, events and places. If we look more closely, however, we may begin to find certain recurring patterns, and by learning to read these patterns we may gain insights into hitherto unacknowledged aspects of ourselves. For example, we may repeatedly seem to attract or be attracted to a particular type of person, even though we may not find these people especially attractive in themselves. A key to understanding why this happens is to be found in the old saying, 'like attracts like'. In other words, the people who come into our lives often serve as a mirror in which we may see more clearly those aspects of ourselves that we have hitherto been unable or unwilling to acknowledge. The same principle may be applied to the events we experience and the situations in which we find ourselves. Once we realize that it is we ourselves who create these underlying patterns, we have a choice: we can either continue to live our lives just as before, or we can use our increased understanding as a means of discarding those aspects of ourselves which impede our personal growth.

The two greatest impediments to personal growth are our tendency to live in the past and our habit of fantasizing about the future. The former causes us to perpetuate the patterns that were established early on in life by rewriting them in the present, while the latter is sometimes little more than a device by which we avoid having to face current reality. The combined effect of these two is that we rarely live life where it is actually happening – now, in the present. One of the functions of the initiatic and mystical traditions is to free us from the constraints imposed upon us by the patterns of our past and our wishful thoughts about the future, thus bringing us into the present. And yet, as many readers will be aware, the Tarot is itself widely used as a tool for looking into the future and for 'fortune telling'.

If you are one of the many who view the Tarot merely as a tool for fortune telling, *The Authentic Tarot* will come as something of a revelation, for within its pages Thomas Saunders debunks this popular but erroneous view. In its place he offers us a series of profound insights into the initiatory function of the Tarot as a key to understanding ourselves and as a tool for personal and/or spiritual growth. To this end he employs what is believed to be the oldest extant complete Tarot deck – the *Ancien Tarot de Marseille* – which is said to date from the 18th century, but the medieval character of the costumes depicted on its cards suggests a much earlier date. The true origins of the Tarot are now obscured by the mists of time, and perhaps it is the very obscurity of its origins that has led in recent decades to the proliferation of new designs for the Tarot. This in itself reveals something about human nature: when we are confronted with something that lies beyond our comprehension, we tend to adapt it – even force it – to fit within the confines of our current level of understanding rather than allow our understanding to be expanded to encompass new and broader horizons.

In reminding us of the ancient initiatic tradition of the Tarot, *The Authentic Tarot* offers us an opportunity to expand our understanding – not only of the Tarot, but also of ourselves. Thomas Saunders' detailed explanation of the traditional imagery of the cards and the significance of each of their symbolic elements provides us with a grammar and vocabulary with which we may begin to read and understand the meaning of the words we write in our book of life. He also transports us into the world of archetypes that people our subconscious minds, thus

offering us insights into previously hidden aspects of our personal consciousness. Moreover, by showing us how to read the Tarot as an
ever-unfolding story, he initiates us into the art of reading the story of
our life so that we may increase our understanding of who we are and
our purpose in being here. In doing so, he has rendered a great service
to us all.

John Baldock

INTRODUCTION

[The Tarot is] a book of knowledge – an encyclopaedia of magical memory images representing a system of mythical wisdom encoded in the pictures.[1]

The Tarot is a *book* of 78 cards telling an ageless story of our journey through life on the path to self-fulfilment. It is told in terms of the Hero's/Heroine's quest to fulfil his or her destiny. The Tarot's deck of cards speaks to us in a covert, symbolic language of archetypal pictographs and numbers; it is an unbound book of illustrations for the teaching of mystical doctrines to those who could not read and write.

An authentic Tarot deck is made up of 22 *Major Arcana* and 56 *Minor Arcana* cards. 'Arcanum' is from the Latin word *arcere* meaning 'to keep'. In English, the word 'arcane' means 'hidden', 'magical' or even 'transcendental'; 'arcana' suggests a secret, a remedy, an elixir or 'having therapeutic value'. Sometimes, the Major Arcana are referred to as Trumps which may be a corruption of the word 'triumphant', meaning to reach one's goal or to reach one's spiritual destiny. 'Arcane' also means something known or understood only by those who have been initiated into a special or secret knowledge: Minor Arcana means 'Lesser secrets' and Major Arcana means 'Greater secrets'.

The Major Arcana comprises 22 cards numbered from I to XXI (1 to 21), and one unnumbered card called The Fool. They have been described as The 22 Steps to Freedom; The Path of the Spiritual Warrior; The Sacred Procession; The Path of Self-Understanding and Self-Realization. The images on the cards depict archetypal characters who represent the stages and pitfalls along a metaphoric pathway that leads from initiation to mastery. They symbolize an allegorical journey through life, expressing the full spectrum of human nature and human endeavour in the language of the soul. (*See* plates 1 and 2.)

The 56 Minor Arcana cards are made up of 14 cards in each of the four 'suits' comprising an ace (number one) and numbers two to ten and the four 'Court' cards – the Knave, the Knight, the Queen and the King. These 56 cards signify the patterns and cycle of events that occur in our everyday life. The four suits are known as Money, Cups, Swords and Clubs, although some decks refer to Money as Pentacles and Clubs as Wands. (*See* plates 6–11.)

The Tarot's images of mythical archetypal characters and numbers mark the milestones that measure our steps as we take courage to journey into the veiled shadows of the mind. Each step forward signals a release from the shackles that restrain us from living by grace and from becoming a fully realized human being. It is a transformational journey from naivety to self-knowledge.

It could be said that the cards are a universal synthesis – an encapsulation – of the archetypal characters and events encountered in the classical myths and fairy tales found throughout the world from ancient history to modern times. Here I am not referring to the myths and fairy tales that have been bowdlerized in mundane adaptations by Walt Disney for Hollywood-style entertainment for children and adults. (Perhaps the one exception is L Frank Baum's modern classic *The Wizard of Oz*, the story of a young girl's spiritual transcendence and psychological maturity. Amazingly, Hollywood did not adapt or change any of the story's inherent symbolism.)

The Tarot is just one of several esoteric teachings based on the perennial story of the psycho/spiritual quest of the Hero or Heroine to become a self-realized human being or, in the words of CG Jung, 'to become that which you already are'. Its profound wisdom charts the milestones and pitfalls we have to encounter and overcome if we choose to progress along our life's path.

To do so, we must recognize and acknowledge these archetypal characters who reside in our unconscious minds and control and manipulate our thought processes and responses. Although each of us experiences these characters in different guises, there are certain processes, responses and aspects of human nature that are common to us all. Of course, we are unconscious of these manipulating, driving forces and the way they govern our behaviour and thoughts but they can be brought to our awareness through the vocabulary of archetypes that are communicated to the conscious mind through dreams, myths, fairy tales, visions, meditations and, of course, the Tarot. The cards show us how we can meet these characters face to face and then enjoy the hidden treasures they have to offer as they deliver profound messages through our innate inner wisdom in a language of ageless symbolism that can light the pathway to 'freedom'.

Every one of us has an insidious, powerful, self-manipulating drive to be loved and to feel wanted. This drive causes us to disregard our instincts, ignore our intuition and do things we positively know we do not want to do. But often we reluctantly agree to do things just to please others in the hope that they will love us, which inevitably leads to resentment. How can we escape from begging others for their unconditional love unless we first graciously accept ourselves – unconditionally? In a sense, it could be said that this is what the modern day psychotherapist does for a client.

As an oracle of perennial wisdom, the Tarot is particularly pertinent to us today. Outwardly, at a conscious level, we live in a one-dimensional fractured society in which:

- honour and ethics in politics and business have been abandoned;
- there is no acceptance of personal responsibility;
- relationships, traditional values and the care and respect for others and Planet Earth have been expediently discarded;
- the profound teachings that have endured throughout the ages go unheeded and unacknowledged;
- the young are left to fend for themselves without any moral or spiritual guidance or sense of personal discipline.

And yet, at a deeper level there is a tangible movement to reach out for a new vision to reconnect ourselves with our selves and the Cosmos. We are searching for some sense of meaning that we hope will further our personal development. And because we cannot seem to find this through the doctrines of orthodox religion, we search for alternative paths to follow that will lead to the top of the same mountain. It is therefore not surprising that ten per cent of all book sales are works on self-development, with young people in particular recognizing that our current pursuit of material goods and our consumerism are at the expense of our inner personal fulfilment.

How can we strengthen our souls to begin such a journey? I believe the Tarot offers one such path.

The Tarot's oracle has invaluable insights to mark out our path and keep us on it: the cards can also be read to help us, the Enquirer – sometimes referred to 'in the trade' as the *Querant* – to tap into our intuitive understanding to deal with and respond to our own, often pressing issues. When we are in *the zone* – in a focused listening mode – the Tarot can put us in touch with our innate knowingness and thus guide us further on the journey towards our fulfilment.

For the cards to be comprehensible and readily understood, a Tarot *Reader* needs to be able to decipher the symbolism of the enigmatic archetypal characters and the sacred meaning of numbers. This means that the Tarot's symbolic language of pictographs and numbers must follow certain conventions of grammar, syntax and vocabulary.

The Tarot is a tool for divination that reveals where we are now standing on *our path through life* and what needs to be the next step forward towards both healing ourselves and further evolving our consciousness. It has the potential to unite and create a balance between the laws that govern the visible world and the laws that govern the invisible world of divine order that transcends our outward experience of the day-to-day events and movements in life. As we learn the Tarot's language we begin to unlock the enigmatic secrets of the cards, and a pattern emerges that can give us clear and precise directions to reach our ultimate destination of self-knowledge and self-realization.

For those new to the Tarot, a typical question might be: 'What can the cards do for me?' This can best be answered by asking another question: 'What do I want in life?' The most common answer to this second question can be summed up as 'leading a happy and fulfilled life' and/or 'self-knowledge'. Everyone will have their own answer but the varied responses could be summed up in the one word *Freedom*. We want freedom to express ourselves; freedom to be creative; freedom to be happy and fulfilled. It could be said that to reach these goals all we need is *Courage*. We need the courage to free ourselves from the conditioning that manipulates every thought and move we make; to free ourselves from the fear of removing the mask of our persona; to free ourselves from egotistical protection and to accept that total, unconditional love is an unrealistic expectation. (However, the Sun does shine unconditionally on both the righteous and the wrongdoers!)

HOW DOES THE TAROT WORK?

When we dream, read a book, see a play or a film, or view a painting, often we can receive extraordinary and important insights. It may be like a lightning flash: suddenly, we have an insight into something of extreme significance to us personally. Others around us will have seen, heard, felt or tasted exactly the same stimulus but for each individual the experience will create a different response. When this happens, something has triggered our intuitive understanding rather than our critical, intellectual mode of thinking. This is how the Tarot can motivate us to take a step towards the next milestone on *our pathway through life*.

Energy follows thought and so, depending upon our willpower, tenacity and commitment, our thoughts can either be fully realized or they can float around in the ether and never come to anything. To realize or manifest something it must first be created in the mind. When we adopt a mental attitude that is both receptive and nonjudgemental, and in which we trust our inner wisdom by listening to our intuition, we open ourselves to receive great insights that can lift us out of the stress of indecision and the feeling of being lost, not knowing what to do or where to go next. Understanding the Tarot can keep us to our path and help us find the answer to the perennial questions: Who am I? Why am I here? What is my destiny?

One of the questions most frequently asked by Tarot sceptics is the matter of random choice. An Enquirer – who from now on will be referred to as the Querant – is asked to shuffle the deck which is already stacked in a haphazard sequence. Under such apparently chaotic conditions, how is it possible for such a random set of cards to have any specific relevance for the person concerned? However, the idea of randomness or coincidence, which may now be explained by the modern, scientific *Theory of Chaos*, was well understood by the ancient seers because they were aware that the Cosmos is governed by a mysterious power of structure and order.

It is said that 'today's mysticism is tomorrow's science'. Bizarre, almost unbelievable facts about our Universe are presented to us by today's hard-nosed physicists. We are told that there are many planes of time and that an electron can be a particle or a wave as well as being in more than one place at the same time. In the subatomic world there are protons and anti-protons that have energy but no mass, which means that a non-mass world interpenetrates the material world we call *reality*. Mystics – those seers who concern themselves with the invisible aspects of reality and its relationship with the reality or *actuality*, visible to us all – were the first to describe these phenomena. Scientists only caught up centuries later when technology evolved and they were able to investigate these happenings 'scientifically'. The Tarot itself acts as a bridge between these two realities – the invisible and the visible. Acceptance of the workings and efficacy of the Tarot is no less a matter of leaping the credibility gap than a general acceptance of current physics concerning time, space, random chance, the unseen worlds of other realities and the oneness of the Universe.

Many psychologists and philosophers such as CG Jung and Rudolf Steiner have written extensively on the transpersonal and spiritual aspects of the meaning of the 22 Major Arcana Tarot cards but have tended not to include the meaning and interpretation of the 56 Minor

Arcana cards. At the other end of the scale there is an extensive range of books that are, more or less, 'teach yourself' manuals on how to read the cards for the sole purpose of fortune telling.

The word *Tarot* can evoke responses that range from the conviction that it is the sinister, malevolent 'work of the Devil' to the view that the cards are nothing more than a harmless after-dinner game for amusement. Others who find the cards enthralling – even magical – are inclined to seek out the fortune tellers in the hope that they can predict how and when they are likely to meet their lover/soul-mate/saviour who will bring about momentous changes to their career/health/wealth, and so on. Ironically, however, if the Tarot is consulted as a means of self-discovery, it can reveal that Miss/Mr 'Right' – the hoped-for perfect lover and benefactor who will change our life and fortune – is not 'out there' but is already residing within us. Although a traumatic experience, an accident, a relationship issue or just simple curiosity can lead a person to consult a Tarot Reader, it is unlikely they will find a pathway to their life's destination by consulting fairground fortune tellers.

Any deck used for fortune telling not only debases the Tarot, it also debases us by its implication that our purpose in being here is for material rather than spiritual fulfilment. Fortune telling takes us into the realm of prediction about future events and thus feeds our expectations, hopes and fears, whereas the Tarot is about taking responsibility for ourselves by dealing with the *here and now* in order for us to take the next step along life's path. In other words, it is about the *present*. With fortune telling, we avoid taking responsibility for ourselves by handing our future over to what someone else predicts it holds for us. Such prediction could possibly invoke a self-fulfilling prophecy. The Tarot Reader can and should act as a facilitator or bridge for the Querant to cross by lifting the veil which, at that moment in their life, prevents them from seeing a particular aspect of themselves. In the right hands, the cards are neither sinister nor malevolent, but in the sense that they appeal to the 'left hand' – our intuitive, instinctive understandings – the cards hold a portentous wisdom to guide us to self-discovery.

There are currently dozens of different Tarot decks and 'Angel'

cards available in bookshops and on the Internet. Unfortunately, most
if not all of those designed over the past 100 years or so are decorated
with highly personalized illustrations that look attractive enough as 'art
for art's sake' but can often either distort or completely ignore the fundamental essence that underlies the arcane meaning of each card that
is intrinsic to the Tarot's language. Some designers even introduce signs
and icons imported from other esoteric systems such as the Kabbalah,
astrology, the Runes and so on which further degrade, corrupt and
obscure the wisdom the authentic Tarot can impart. Of course, it is
immaterial whether the design of a Tarot deck is of ancient or modern
origin, provided that the integrity of the established precepts and
accepted conventions of the Tarot's 'language' in terms of grammar,
vocabulary and syntax – i.e. the orderly or systematic arrangement of
the various elements – is adhered to in the symbolic pictographs. If any
language, whether verbal or pictorial, is not rational and logical then
there is little chance anyone will be able to understand what is being
conveyed.

Probably the most popular modern deck used by the majority of
Tarot teachers is the *Rider Waite*, conceived by AE Waite and designed
by Pamela Colman Smith in 1910. I too was taught the Tarot with this
deck several years ago and gradually learned off by heart the Rider
Waite interpretations of each of the 78 cards. Undoubtedly the illustrations are explicit and, after a time, easy to remember. But as with
other relatively modern decks, they tend to express the designer's
subjective, sometimes spurious and usually 'New Age' interpretations
which pay no regard to the integrity of the ancient system. For many
years I read spreads according to the rather rigid definitions for each
card that were dictated by various teachers, and I have to admit that I
used these definitions in my private readings and during a three-year
period when I was the Tarot Reader for *Marie Claire* magazine and
broadcasting on LBC Radio London. Since then I have come to realize
that the meanings attributed to the Rider Waite and several other
decks are not entirely in accord with the fundamental, sacred wisdom
embedded in the enigmatic pictographs and numbers of an authentic
Tarot deck.

One of the oldest complete sets of Tarot cards was published by BP Grimaud in 1769. Known as the *Ancien Tarot de Marseille*, it depicts costumes and decorations that can be dated back to at least the early 14th century. This deck has been used throughout this book because the symbolism of both the pictographs and the numbers follows the conventions of a comprehensible language not found in other packs. By contrast, it may also serve as a response to the plethora of 'designer' Tarot packs with their whimsical illustrations and introduction of various other divinatory systems and symbolisms.

When I came across the *Marseille* deck a few years ago, I was at first surprised and puzzled by the diagrams/patterns that differentiate each suit and which particularly appealed to me as a student of sacred symbolism and the ancient, esoteric meaning and interpretation of the numbers one to ten. Delving further, it became obvious that all the pictographs of the Major and Minor Court cards in the *Marseille* deck had been designed using a common bond that unifies all the cards into one, co-ordinated symbolic system. In other words, the colours, clothing, postures, weapons and other artefacts illustrated in the pictographs and the sacred meanings of the numbers are *grammatically* consistent and correct. This creates a cohesiveness and rationality to enable us to comprehend the imparted wisdom. Studying the Tarot is, at first, like trying to learn a foreign language but gradually we can become familiar with all the subtleties and nuances of interpretation. It also became clear that an 'authentic' deck – by this I don't just mean one that is several centuries old – such as the *Marseille* pack has a profound depth of wisdom that, hitherto, I had not begun to fully understand even though, as mentioned above, I had been reading the Tarot for several years previously.

My intention in writing this book is not only to respond to the current widespread use of the Tarot as little more than a system for fortune telling, but also to re-establish the cards as a tool to provide us with insights into the hidden workings of the mind, thus enlightening us as to why we do the things we do, why we attract certain people into our lives, and why certain events in our lives seem to keep repeating themselves.

Writing a book about the Tarot inevitably requires deciphering the allegorical input of the 78 cards and their specific, individual meanings or symbolic expression. The pitfall is that the very criticism levelled at other decks that they express the designers' very personal interpretations of the cards could be levelled at anyone who submits their own – again subjective – interpretations.

In an attempt to be objective and circumspect, I have offered an interpretation of the graphic symbolism by drawing the reader's attention to the detail in each of the 22 Major and the 16 Court cards of the Minor Arcana. I have also set out what may be considered to be a consensus of the universally accepted esoteric meanings of the card numbers one to ten for each of the four suits. These personal suggestions are not put forward as 'the truth' but merely 'a likely story', with the intention of leaving the Tarot student and Reader with a wide scope for their own insights and perceptions to be explored.

This book attempts to decipher the language symbolism to show how the pictographs and numbers can reveal some of the hidden secrets of our human nature, as well as showing how the cards can be read without resorting to prediction or the forecasting of some future event. It invites experienced Tarot Readers and teachers to review and compare the symbolism and applied meanings of the pictographs in whatever pack they are currently using. It is also written as an introduction for newcomers to the Tarot and will, I believe, appeal to both beginners and those with some knowledge of the cards. Primarily, it is intended as a practical guide for those who are consciously travelling along a path searching for their *truth and meaning of life* which might best be discovered through myths and symbols that draw us toward an infinite unity.

TAROT THROUGH
THE AGES

The origins of the Tarot are as mysterious as the Tarot itself. Esoteric teachings throughout the ages have been a strictly oral tradition, but with the advent of the printed word it became necessary to create a system that covertly preserved the ancient initiatory knowledge – the Tarot. Speculations about the precise origins of the cards tend to be more or less regurgitated in most books about the Tarot but is it really of any great concern? Perhaps for some people, setting the date as early as possible – the Atlantean Age or Ancient Egypt – gives special credence to its authenticity and luminosity. Let's just say it was devised 'once upon a time'.

It seems the first positively identified Tarot scholar of significance was Antoine Court de Gébelin, a French archaeologist, who in the late 18th century pronounced that the cards had originated in Egypt, but the source of his information is not clear. Whatever their origin, the popular opinion is that the cards came from somewhere other than Europe itself. Unfortunately, we Westerners tend to revere and favour the philosophies and religions of Asia and the Middle East rather than respect and treasure our own rich European esoteric traditions. Why do we find Taoism, Buddhism, the Chinese system of *Feng Shui* and the similar Indian system of *Vastu Shastra* (meaning House Science) more interesting than our own equivalent and equally profoundly erudite culture such as the Celtic tradition which has, or had, a far greater relevance to our Western way of life?

A popular conception is that the Gypsies, who originated not in Egypt but in India, introduced the cards into Europe and used them for fortune telling, but current evidence indicates that the Indians arrived in the West about a century or more after the first Tarot cards appeared in France and Italy. ('Tarocchi' is an old Italian gambling game of cards). Others suggest the cards were brought into Spain from the Middle East by the Saracens or the Crusaders. It could be just as likely that the Tarot originated from the Medieval Rosicrucians, although they may have adapted it from an earlier tradition.

Of course, it would certainly be interesting if, one day, an archae-ologist/historian/researcher did discover the origins of the Tarot. However, although the knowledge of when and whence it came might satisfy the curiosity of those who enjoy such academic certainties, to my mind a more important question is whether a deck – either ancient or modern – expresses the sacred concepts, esoteric teachings and integrity of the symbolic language of the Tarot.

According to the *Woman's Encyclopaedia of Myths and Secrets* by Barbara G Walker, the world's oldest gambling game is called Faro or 'the game of kings'. Spain's national card game Ombre – 'the game of Man' – was as much a system of mystical divination as a modified version of an earlier game, Primero, which most resembled the ancient Tarot. The cards have also been called the 'game of re-birth' and 'a compendium of gypsy philosophy and religion'.[1]

Undoubtedly, the history of religious dogma and persecution has caused the more so-called 'Pagan' esoteric teachings to go under-ground. In the case of the Tarot, the Christian priesthood attacked the use of the cards, and even today many people and church authorities are afraid of the Tarot's occult connotations. The apparently benign reason why the Christian Church objected to the Tarot and to card playing generally was that such pastimes were thought to be frivolous and could lead to gambling. But it is more likely that the cards were banned because, through a combination of ignorance and religious intolerance, they were thought to express the various guises or aspects of evil and idolatry invented by the Devil.

The Tarot has been recognized as a powerful tool for the self-discovery of one's inner, intuitive spiritual knowledge or *gnosis*. ('Gnosis' means 'an intuitive experience and understanding of esoteric truths – an inner wisdom'.) Orthodox religions cannot tolerate an individual's intuitive feelings or a personal search for mystical experiences, and so the early Christian Gnostics were hunted down and almost wiped out because they wanted to experience for themselves an 'inner godliness' rather than follow a blind belief in religious dogma. As the saying goes, 'the religious man believes; the mystic knows'. The Greek philosopher Plato (429–347 BCE) held the view that everyone is gifted with complete wisdom and knowledge and the true teacher is one who simply helps us to *remember* that which intuitively and instinctively we already know! Indeed, the Tarot was intended to be, and in the right hands can be, a 'true teacher' that leads to self-knowledge and spiritual enlightenment.

In his book *Researches into the History of Playing Cards*, published in London in 1816, Samuel Weller Singer suggests that the Tarot cards were part of the magical and philosophical lore secured by the Knights Templar from the Saracens or one of the mystical sects in Syria. To avoid persecution when they returned to Europe, the Knights Templar concealed the symbolic meanings by pretending the cards were for gambling. Although the Templars, who had been founded in Jerusalem in 1119, were condemned as heretics and cruelly suppressed in 1312 by the Papacy who feared their power, the Tarot survived. In his book *The Secret Teachings of All Ages*, Manly P Hall tells us that in 1370, a monk called John Brefeld said that in the symbolism of the cards "'the state of the world as it is now is most excellently described and figured.'" Hall goes on to say, '… this too was considered to be heretical and from the 14th century onwards the Tarot cards were denounced as *The Devil's Books*.'[2]

By the 14th and 15th centuries, the Church had become extremely intolerant of other traditions and sects such as the Jews and the Cathars, who were the last vestiges of the early Christian Gnostics. The Tarot was forbidden throughout Italy and France, and in Germany packs were burned. Nuremberg and Tournai (Belgium) – where the card painters were mainly women – witnessed scenes of some of the worst witch hunts in Europe.

Surprisingly, during the same period of extreme intolerance the nomadic Gypsies used the Tarot to express their own occult, spiritual beliefs centred around the Great Mother Matriarchal principle personified by the Pagan Mother Earth Goddess Tara, who ruled the fate of men. The name has other similar derivations in the Greek, Roman, Indian and Celtic traditions which Barbara Walker suggests is the origin of the name *Tarot*.[3]

The earliest known record of the Tarot cards being produced in the West dates from 1392. The cards – 15 Major Arcana and 2 Minor Arcana – are preserved in the Bibliothèque Nationale in Paris. No one can tell how many there may have been in the full deck but they can be accurately dated because the French King Charles VI's treasurer recorded a cash payment to an artist Jacquemin Gringonneur for painting three decks. About 30 years later, there is another record of an Italian painter Bonifacio Bembo who painted a deck for the Duke of Milan, but again it appears that not all the cards survived. The earliest complete set of Tarot cards, published in 1769 and known as the *Ancien Tarot de Marseille*, illustrates costumes and decorations which could be dated back to the early 14th century, before the Gringonneur cards were painted.

Unless Gringonneur was not only an artist but also a mystic who received the divine wisdom of the 78 cards by means of channelled inspiration from the ether – which of course is possible – someone must have produced an extant deck of cards for him to copy or adapt. If this is the case, it would suggest that the Tarot cards were in existence in Europe much earlier than the 14th century.

The costumes of the Major Arcana and the Minor Arcana Court cards of the *Ancien Tarot de Marseille* authentically illustrate the clothing and armour of the period of Medieval Europe between about 1300 and 1450.[4] (*See* plates 1, 2 and 8–11.) Shorter beards and long-pointed shoes were also in fashion in the mid-14th century. In fact, the extraordinary length of shoes became the subject of an Act of Parliament in 1388 which 'prohibited the making of shoes with toes exceeding two inches beyond the necessary convenience of walking.' Nor were the multi-coloured parbaloons, or close-fitting leggings, as we now call them, any less absurd. The costumes also closely resemble the pageant dresses of the early mystery plays.[5]

In his book *The Mystical Tower of the Tarot*, JD Blakely says that, according to Paul Marteau, 'the ancient Marseille pack is a reproduction of the arrangement which was edited in 1761 by Nicolas Conver, maître cartier of Marseilles who had conserved the wood (blocks) and colours of his distant predecessors, but no date is given for their origin.'[6]

Over the centuries, costumes, styles and fashions have changed the designs of the cards, but it would seem the basic format and integrity of the Tarot remained intact until the 19th century when Alphonse Louis Constant (1810–75), a Roman Catholic Abbé and herbalist, wrote *Transcendental Magic* under the pseudonym Eliphas Lévi Zahed (or simply, Eliphas Lévi). The book expounded on the correspondences between the 22 letters and numbers of the Hebraic alphabet and the 22 Major Arcana cards of the Tarot. Although there are 22 cards, The Fool is numbered 'zero', which immediately creates a discrepancy between the numbering of the Hebraic letters and the numbering of the cards. Such spurious discrepancies have to be fudged over, which only serves to obscure the full impact and meaning of the Tarot's unique symbolism. However, Eliphas Lévi did profoundly say, 'An imprisoned person with no other book than the Tarot, if he knew how to use it, could in a few years acquire universal knowledge and would be able to speak on all subjects with unequalled learning and inexhaustible eloquence.'

Since Lévi, other 19th and 20th century occultists – notably Aleister Crowley and AE Waite of the Order of the Golden Dawn – and many more French, American and British authors have produced elaborate tables which deceptively claim to show how numerology, Kabbalah, the I Ching, the astrological signs, the Runes, musical notes, colours, gems, animals, plants, magical weapons and perfume have a direct metaphysical correspondence with the Tarot. Some packs have even expanded the number of the Major Arcana to as many as 40 cards!

Such attempts to attribute astrological signs to the Tarot have also created a wide diversity of opinion resulting in a confused interpretation of the cards. This is particularly so in the case of Major Arcana card numbers VIII and XI. If the *Marseille* deck is generally accepted as being the most authentic and certainly the oldest known complete set, it places Judgement at Number VIII and Force at Number XI. (Force is illustrated by a person staring into the open jaws of a lion.) Most modern decks, particularly the *Ryder Waite* pack, place Force or Strength at Number VIII because the sign of Leo (represented by a lion) is in the eighth house of the Zodiac and this led to the interchange of numbers VIII and XI. As we shall see later, placing the cards according to the *Marseille* deck where Judgement is Number VIII creates a logical sequence of steps on the Path to Fulfilment. Another 'fudging' of the Tarot symbolism occurs when cards are attributed with the personality characteristics of certain signs of the Zodiac, such as suggesting that Major Arcana card Number VI The Lover expresses the traits of a Gemini or that card Number IV The Emperor personifies an Aries Sun sign.

Imposing changes to the numbered sequence of the cards to coincide with personal ideas about astrological or Kabbalistic correspondences or the inclusion of additional symbolism in the design of a card simply corrupts the fundamental wisdom of the Tarot. Each divinatory or oracular system uses its own unique method for charting the steps to self-awareness and enlightenment, but the pathways leading to the goal of one's quest pass through different territories in much the same manner that the spiritual teachings of every religion follow a well-defined and yet seemingly separate road to reach the same mountain of enlightenment and personal destiny. The Vedas tell us, 'Truth is one, the sages speak of it by many names.' As we shall see later, however, the esoteric symbolism of numbers – in particular the numbers one to ten – certainly has correlations and a common bond with other occult systems in which the number, geometry and rhythm of the Cosmos resonates with the cycles and happenings in the life of a person.

Apart from their common bond of number symbolism (as opposed to Numerology), the quest of the 20th-century occultists to produce a *Grand Unifying Theory* that binds all these occult traditions into one homogenous, conglomerate and interchangeable system may be as fruitless as the long-sought-after unified theory of physics. Stephen Hawking, one of the world's foremost cosmologists and theoretical physicists, questions whether there can ever be a unified theory or is this simply a mirage? In his book *A Brief History of Time*, Hawking says that 'some would argue … that if there were a complete set of laws, that would infringe God's freedom to change his mind and intervene in the world.'[7]

Of course, the Tarot is a living language but it is hoped that in the 21st century we have now gone beyond the phase of trying to unify it with the symbolism of other esoteric traditions. Of course, it would be unreasonable to suggest that the *Marseille* pack was the *one and only* authentic, uncorrupted replica of the original symbolism of earlier decks: no doubt through the ages, variations have been and will continue to be introduced by those who feel the need to make changes to suit their own interpretations and insights. But if the designers of such cards have misinterpreted or misunderstood the arcane meanings of the Tarot, the wisdom will be distorted and obscured. As Richard Feynman (1918–88), the American physicist and Nobel Prize winner, wisely said, 'You can recognize Truth by its beauty and simplicity.'

To understand the Tarot we must decipher the symbolism, but first we must ensure that the Tarot deck we are using has a logical and comprehensive set of symbols that are compatible throughout the whole pack of cards otherwise the full import is lost or, at worst, the 'language' is confusing and unreadable. In other words, the symbolic grammar, vocabulary and syntax must be consistent and follow a logical pattern. The *Ancien Tarot de Marseille* deck by BP Grimaud satisfies such 'rules' and has a rationality which ensures that the symbols combine with each other in a relationship that is both coherent and meaningful. The introduction of signs or sigils imported from other esoteric traditions and systems is akin to, say, reading a European language such as German or French and suddenly finding a Japanese ideogram or an Arabic script interspersed in the text. Such foreign language words would be incomprehensible and meaningless.

Unless the integrity of the system remains intact, the quality, profundity and clarity of the interpretation will be compromised and may lead the reader to miss the mark. When the unique symbolism underpinning the Tarot is read as a stand-alone oracle of sacred wisdom, without any extraneous embellishments associated with other systems or traditions, our psyche will be able to receive a clear, unambiguous message.

2

THE MYTHICAL JOURNEY OF THE HERO/HEROINE

The steps marking the *pathway to self-knowledge* are expressed in the Major Arcana cards in deep and layered symbols that bring to life the intrinsic detail and meaning of each step forward. Self-knowledge is the discovery not of the 'I' but the 'Self'. In the broadest of terms, our heroic journey of initiation begins as a child flowing with life: we are loved, blessed and, for many of us, we may even be in a state of blissful naivety.

In terms of the Tarot, at the beginning we are The Fool who embodies our primordial state of naivety. At the end of our Tarot journey we are still The Fool but older and wiser, having gradually emerged like a butterfly from its chrysalis cocoon. Although there are variations to the symbolism, the Tarot's 21 steps on the path of initiation are more or less the foundation of many of the classical myths. Whatever the cultural or ethnic source – European, Scandinavian, Middle Eastern, Asian, North or South American, and so on throughout the World – universally, the myths fundamentally follow the same underlying themes.

As we shall see in chapter 7, 'Reading a Spread', the Heroic rite of passage from unconscious naivety to fulfilment runs in three segments: Separation, Initiation and the Return. Joseph Campbell outlines this rite of passage in his book *The Hero with a Thousand Faces* where he tells us 'a hero [or heroine] ventures forth from the world of common day into a [dark] region of supernatural wonder where fabulous [and dangerous] forces are encountered and a decisive victory is won; the hero [or heroine] comes back from his mysterious adventure with the power to bestow boons on his fellow man.'[1]

Before the advent of 20th-century psychotherapy, guidance for self-awareness and our spiritual journey came from the archetypal characters in the classical myths and fairy tales – the evil giants, wicked witches, good fairies, wise old men and women, monsters, caves and mysterious happenings or interventions. They tell us how we can face up to and overcome the overwhelming trials and fierce ordeals we will inevitably encounter on our own heroic journey from child-like or childish immaturity to the golden chalice of self-realization. These traditional archetypes, who may epitomize some of the sub-personalities hidden in the shadows of our mind, are similar to the characters we will meet in the Tarot's rite of passage.

What is this heroic journey we must undertake to fulfil our quest for self-knowledge? At a mundane level, myths and fairy tales may be viewed simply as well-devised stories written to entertain or even frighten children in an attempt to warn them of life's hazards. At another level, the tales would be viewed as symbolic expressions of the primal nature of human beings which direct us toward what CG Jung called 'individuation' – our destiny to become self-realized. At the mystical level, the stories tend to be interpreted as a portrayal of soul experiences and universal spiritual truths.

Myths and fairy tales such as Parsifal searching for the holy grail (a symbol of his own redemption), Iron John's struggle with himself, Dorothy's liberation in *The Wizard of Oz* and so on, are all about a heroic journey ending in rebirth and deliverance. In many other tales the journey ends in a happy-ever-after marriage – the wedding being the integration of the masculine and feminine principles that will transform our life. We can see how the integration of these two principles works in the stories of Theseus and the Minotaur and the fairy tale of Jack and the Beanstalk.

The myth of Theseus and the Minotaur tells us that when Theseus was 16 years old he was strong enough to lift a rock to retrieve his father's sandals and sword. He then went on his warrior-like travels, slaying bandits, criminals and monsters. When he arrived in Athens he heard about the Minotaur – a beast with the body of a monstrous animal and the head of a man – it has bestial instincts and is clever with it! It lived in a deep underground labyrinth where it was fed on the flesh of young men and women. Theseus was prepared to kill the beast but knew that, once inside the cavernous tunnels, he could find his way to the Minotaur but would not be able to find his way back. Then along came his lover Ariadne who gave him a ball of string (sometimes a golden thread) which he could trail behind him to retrace his steps back to the light of day.

Theseus knew he was capable of slaying the beast, but without Ariadne's thread he would remain imprisoned in the labyrinth for the rest of his life.

In this story Theseus personifies the *Masculine* Principle – rationality, instinctiveness and activity – all to do with the 'head'. Ariadne personifies the *Feminine* Principle – intuition, feelings and passivity – all to do with the 'heart'. These principles are attributes, if you will, and whether we are male or female they are present in all of us to some greater or lesser degree.

The Minotaur personifies the basic instincts within Theseus himself. The labyrinth is the deep recesses of his unfathomable, unconscious mind which will be referred to later as the *shadow*.

The discovery of his father's sandals and sword tells us that he is old enough to begin his own journey and carry a weapon – his manhood. He embarks on a crusade against the evils of the world when he hears about the Minotaur, which, we are told, only feeds off the young flesh of virgins. (It is surprising the victims never worked out how to beat that particular problem!) In other words, the beast exists purely for sensuous gratification. The Minotaur lives in the deep underground labyrinth of our hero's mind.

Theseus knows he is capable of slaying the Minotaur – he can suppress his own basic instincts – but unless he can bring these controlling traits to the surface of his conscious mind he will never escape these negative aspects of his personality. Ariadne – the Feminine Principle – provides him with the golden thread to guide him back to the light of consciousness and enlightenment.

This myth tells us that whatever our 'beasts' may be, merely suppressing them will not lead us further on the path to self-knowledge. But if we accept and recognize them, we will achieve a dynamic balance between the Masculine and Feminine Principles within ourself.

In the story of Jack and the Beanstalk, his mother tells him the cow has gone dry and he must take it to sell in the market. On his way, he meets an old man who persuades him to sell the cow for five beans. When Jack returns his mother is furious and throws the beans out of the window. They grow into a huge beanstalk that reaches up to the sky. Jack climbs up and discovers a giant and his wife who are guarding a goose that lays golden eggs. While the giant is away his wife shows Jack how to take a golden egg.

In telling us that the cow has gone dry, the story indicates that Jack can no longer be dependent on being looked after at home. (Perhaps unwittingly, Jack's mother does what all mothers should do – she tells her son he must now fend for himself and not be tied to her!)

On his care-free way to market, Jack meets an old (i.e. wise) man who exchanges seemingly worthless beans for the cow. This is Jack's first act of disobedience, marking his independence from his mother and, inevitably, she shows her fury, as most mothers do, on realizing that her son is no longer under her control. Instead, his intuition guided him to heed the wise old man. The beans represent Jack's as yet unrealized talents and abilities. The growth of the beanstalk is a phallic symbol personifying his own growing maturity where only the sky is the limit to his potentialities. But when he climbs up it he discovers that the goose that lays the golden eggs – unlimited abundance – is guarded by a fierce giant who lives there with his wife. Again, as with the story of Theseus, the giant is the monster – Jack's basic instinct – and it is the giant's wife (the Feminine Principle) who shows Jack how to get hold of the eggs. The beanstalk is a means for Jack to rise up to the heavenly, spiritual realms.

Jack's goal – unknown at the beginning of the journey – is to find the precious eggs. This goal is sometimes referred to in other stories as the crock of gold, the Holy Grail or an alchemical substance: these are metaphors for our soul or the inner essence of our being. The tipping point that triggers a boy's first step on the path occurs at the moment when he defies his mother and follows his instinct.

Perhaps one of the finest examples of the tipping point for a girl is found in the classical myth of Psyche and Amor, which is a complete and most valuable study of the psychological and spiritual development of the feminine. The story is taken from the second-century Roman classic *The Golden Ass* by Apuleius. Amor (also known as Cupid or Eros), a mischievous and immature 'boy', was the son of Aphrodite (also known as Venus) the goddess of love, beauty and sensuality. Psyche, a mortal princess, at first obeyed her father's order that she should be offered as a sacrifice to the gods, but Fate intervened and she left the family home. She then succumbed to the amorous attentions of Amor, but his mother Aphrodite (her future mother-in-law!) felt usurped and wreaked her cruel revenge on Psyche by imposing on her the most horrendous ordeals. Through instinct, intuition, tenacity and, finally, by following the wise guidance of the animated Tower – a symbol for the core of her being – she survived the ordeals. Finally, through the love of a now mature Amor, Psyche was transformed into an immortal goddess. (*Psyche* was the Greek word for the soul.)[2]

As we can see, nothing is as it appears to be on the surface and everything has an underlying or inner meaning or, put another way: *As above, so below.*

THE JOURNEY BEGINS

> The Tarot has been described as 'an outline of initiation,
> and as some form of initiation has formed the heart of
> every World religion, the truths contained in the Tarot
> symbolism are universal and belong to no one race, creed
> or culture, but constitute a text book for every serious
> aspirant on the Path of Light.'[3]

The Hero or Heroine's first step on the path is usually triggered by a
sense of longing, of boredom, perhaps a desire to rescue someone/
something or an experience of an unusual occurrence. Sometimes this
is known as *the call to adventure*.

What Prevents Us From Embarking on Such a Journey?

When confronted with the decision about whether to take the first step
on the Tarot's Path of the Initiate – the way of the Hero or Heroine
– we can either retreat into the eternal round of material gratification
and ego trips where we are controlled and manipulated by the forces
of our unconscious mind, or we can make the commitment and
resolve to set out on our quest to satisfy our inner yearnings to become
whole, complete, fulfilled and to transcend the unconscious human
condition. As we shall see later, what deters us is *fear*.

Every day we are faced with having to make choices from the
options we perceive to be available. Struggling with indecision can
dissipate our energies. In the words of the American Protestant
theologian, Reinhold Niebuhr (1892–1971), 'God, grant me the serenity
to accept the things I cannot change, the courage to change the things
I can, and the wisdom to know the difference.'

The word 'decide' has the same root as infanticide, suicide, and
homicide: it means 'to kill off'. In other words, when we decide on a
course of action it means we have eliminated/killed off the other
options which then allows all our energy to be focused on a single goal.

Of course, every decision, however minor or major, will have consequences but ultimately every decision we make will be based on either love or fear. If the choice is made out of love – the 'self-love' relating to our self-esteem – it will be positive, in the light, and will progress our spiritual endeavour. (The love referred to here is not about erotic love or loved ones but concerns the respect, compassion and spiritual love for oneself – one's soul – that transcends the ego-centred 'I'.) If we choose out of fear, the consequences will be negative, dark and constricting to the spirit.

Alan J Lerner, the late American lyricist who wrote such poetic words for *My Fair Lady*, *Camelot* and many others, presented a Masterclass on his art and dramatic writing at the New York Athletic Club in the early 1990s. He said that in all good theatre, the first act sets the scene for conflict: without conflict there is no drama! This tells us about the Hero or Heroine, or as we now call them the Protagonists. In the second act, the protagonist is confronted by challenging, even life-threatening forces that threaten to overwhelm him or her. If the protagonist is a character who, like Hamlet, succumbs and is defeated by those forces then the drama becomes a tragedy. If, however, the protagonist is someone like Rosalind in *As You Like It*, who confronts, resists and overcomes the powerful forces against her, then the drama becomes a comedy.

Day by day, we can all face conflicts: some may be of little import and others could be rather more threatening, but always we have to decide whether 'to suffer the slings and arrows of outrageous fortune or, by opposing, end them'.[4]

By opposing the overwhelming forces the Hero or Heroine becomes a 'spiritual warrior': one who never reacts but only takes action on his or her own terms; one who cannot be provoked into action but remains calm as if in meditation, yet still acutely alert at all times; one who has 360° vision – the ability to see even where he or she is not looking; one who never threatens or rattles the sword as a warning, but when the weapon is drawn is prepared to kill and, more importantly, is prepared to be killed. The true Hero knows when to advance and when to retreat and, unlike the immature Hero in shining armour (The Fool in his state of naivety), he does not rely on 'luck' or some romantic notion that 'all will be well'. A spiritual warrior is a calculated risk taker – not a gambler – and never acts in anger. The evolved Hero or Heroine is a person of compassion and love who will live by goodness, beauty and truth.

There is a story of a Samurai warrior whose brother was murdered. After seeking the murderer for several years, the Samurai found the killer and as he was about to dispatch him the killer spat in his face. The Samurai sheathed his sword, knowing he could not kill the man in anger.

How do we begin this journey on the 'path to self-fulfilment'? From time to time, perhaps more often when a crisis or trauma has occurred, we may be nudged by a sense of gentle pressure on the nape of the neck or a somewhat strange, persistently aching 'gut-feeling' that is telling us we need to do something to change direction or to set out on our own 'heroic journey'. Sometimes it comes in the form of an accident or illness; sometimes it comes to us in our quiet moments of solitude and introspection. To seek answers demands the Hero's pre-requisite qualities of courage, commitment and tenacity.

THE ORDEALS OF THE HERO/HEROINE

On the journey there are many trials and overwhelming forces that have to be confronted: there are dragons to slay, dark powers to fight, fatigue and despair to overcome and a retreat into a cave to seek solitude where the *shadow* is encountered and the Hero or Heroine realizes that whatever the treasures may be they will be difficult to search for, discover and keep.

The ordeals of the Hero or Heroine correspond to the process of *initiation* in which we face the *shadow* – that is, face our *complexes*. These complexes, most of which appear to have been inherited conditioning from an early age, control us and hold us in their thrall. 'Facing the *shadow*' marks the moment when we begin to understand what we have to do to discover our own innate wisdom and knowledge.

The Shadow

When we find ourselves 'hating' someone, breathing forceful vengeance and revenge, it is the moment to look inside and understand that the person who is the subject of our attack is more than likely a mirror image of an aspect of our own nature. As we shall see below, we tend to become that which we hate! Of course, we need to exercise discernment whenever we find ourselves either disliking or approving of someone or something. But when judgement and criticism are accompanied by anger and rage, we are then projecting our own faults onto others. If we refuse to recognize the reality of our own being, it will continue to torment us. As we are so acutely aware of the negativity in others because it strikes a chord within our self, by the same token we cannot recognize the positive qualities in others unless we too possess those same attributes: we could not speak of concepts such as love, compassion, kindness and other qualities unless we were aware of those qualities within our self. To test this, ask yourself, 'What is it that I most *like* about my partner/spouse/best friend/colleague?' And then ask yourself 'What is it that I most *dislike* about my partner/spouse/best friend/colleague?' Ironically, whatever it is you most dislike is that which you most need to recognize and understand about yourself.

We can recognize the *shadow* working in others when we see, for example, a person who gets married and then divorces only to later get married again to someone who has almost the same distinctive characteristics as the person they first married. What is the alchemy of attraction that brings us together with our partner? Is it the pheromones, the glance, the voice from 'across a crowded room' that makes us fall in lust and form a relationship or is this the *shadow* in action? At an unconscious level it is our respective psyches in collaboration. The object of our desire mirrors an aspect of our *shadow* that needs to evolve into consciousness. And so the two psyches say, 'she looks good, he feels good, she smells good,' and so on to get the juices flowing that will keep a couple together for however long is necessary. After a time, a couple can acknowledge the reason they are together and understand that all the traumas and the so called 'ups and downs' of a marriage/partnership are a manifestation of our natural reluctance to learn the relevant lessons, and be prepared to accept that our chosen partner is doing a perfect job by helping us to gradually discover a little more about our self. Alternatively, if they resist heeding the lessons and reject these golden opportunities to move on, they will be drawn like a magnet to a new partner who will be teaching them exactly the same lesson, except that the experience will get harder and become more traumatic. Ultimately, if we are willing to face them, we can begin to get to grips with the hidden and often self-destructive forces that control us.

Interestingly, what we are supposed to learn at school are the three Rs: Reading, 'Riting and 'Rithmetic, but in the outside world we learn Resistance, Resentment and Revenge!

To illustrate how the *shadow* exerts unseen pressures on our life we can take the example of the dependency manifested by abused men and women. How is it that a person who has been the victim of abuse as a child often finds him or herself in a partnership or marriage with an abuser? Surely, anyone who has suffered abuse as a child would instinctively steer well clear of anyone who is likely to abuse them in their adult life. And yet at every Alcoholics Anonymous and Narcotics Anonymous meeting there will be many *dependants* – spouses and partners of the abusers – who have a history of being abused.

This is the *shadow's* way to guide us towards self-healing. Our progress along the path of life is governed not only by the way we respond to the people we meet and draw into our lives, but also by our response to external events. If we were made redundant, for example, would we consider this to be the worst thing that could possibly happen to us, or would we look on it as an opportunity to make significant changes in our life? And who's to say that in some mysterious manner, somehow, unconsciously we may have manipulated the chain of events to instigate the apparently unfortunate outcome of being rejected or sacked?

A most erudite definition of the *shadow* can be found in Thorwald Dethlefsen and Rüdiger Dahlke's book, *The Healing Power of Illness*. They suggest that whenever we try to identify ourselves by what we do and what we think – for example, 'I am tolerant', 'I am spiritually minded', 'I am hard working', and so on – we set up conflicting value judgements about who we are. In doing so, we immediately exclude all the things we don't want to be or are afraid of discovering about our selves – namely, that we are intolerant, materialistic, lazy and so on. Instead, we project what we perceive to be these unpleasant or undesirable traits onto other people 'out there'.

According to Dethlefsen and Dahlke, shadow creatures do not always remain in the psychological realm: whilst they may be unrecognized, sooner or later they will manifest themselves in the body as symptoms of illness. They go on to say:

> What we concern ourselves with most is what we do not want … [The] 'outer' world acts as a mirror in which all that we ever see is ourselves – and in particular our shadow, to which we are otherwise inwardly blind. We are partially blind to our own psyche, and are capable of recognizing the part of it that is invisible to us (the shadow) only via its projection and reflection in the supposed environment or 'outer' world. Those who inhabit this world without recognizing that everything they perceive and experience is *none other than themselves* are entangled in a web of deception and illusion. … Yet exactly the contrary is actually the case; the shadow contains everything that the world – our world – most needs for its salvation and healing. The shadow makes us ill – *un-well* – because it is the very thing that is lacking for our *well-being*. For this reason every mythical hero desirous of becoming both healed and healer has had to come to grips with horrors, dragons, demons and even hell itself.[5]

When we banish what we consider to be our negative traits, they do not go away. They become embedded in the unconscious mind, but – inevitably and when least expected – they will emerge unwelcomed from the *shadow* and manifest themselves in our daily life.

THE HERO/HEROINE'S RETURN

When there is a resolve to continue the journey, the Hero or Heroine emerges from the cave and out of the shadow into the light (of consciousness). This re-birth or resurrection, which carries with it the prospect of complete mastery of ourselves – body, mind and spirit – is known as the *return*. In fairy tales, this mastery is often represented by the wedding that brings many such tales to an end.

Becoming a Man or Woman of Knowledge

In Carlos Castaneda's book *The Teachings of Don Juan,* Don Juan, a Mexican Indian shaman, speaks about the 'enemies' we will encounter before we can become 'a man [woman] of knowledge'. He says that when we set out on our quest to learn about ourselves we have no clear perception of our objectives, nor of the hardships the quest will entail.[6]

At some point in our lives we set out to explore and learn something about the 'occult' or hidden mysteries. For some of us this may simply be an inner need to find the answers to life's perennial questions. No doubt, the process of seeking the answers will be challenging and often fearful the more we journey into the unknown.

The first enemy we will encounter is Fear, but if we turn away from it our life can become harmless and ineffective. Dispelling the fear leads to the second enemy, what Castaneda calls Clarity of Mind, through which we may become assured and courageous. But if this newly-acquired sense turns into a feeling of invincibility, it will block our pathway to further learning and understanding to the point where we become the immature crusader of lost causes or take on the guise of a clown – the naïve Fool – or, at worst, we can turn into a tyrant.

Having attained clarity of mind, we will then meet our third enemy Power, which can blind us and divert us from pursuing our quest for learning. At this point, the danger is that we may come to the end of our life without ever understanding our selves and the world about us.

By defeating these three enemies, we have no more fears: our clarity of mind and the self-control over power mean that we are almost at the end of our quest, but we must now confront the last enemy – Old Age. This is a battle we can and must fight while knowing that we can never win. Don Juan tells Castaneda that if we give in to tiredness or yearn to rest we will become feeble and lose our clarity, power and knowledge. But, he says, if he 'lives his fate [and does not succumb to tiredness] … he can be called a man of knowledge, if only for a brief moment when he succeeds in fighting off his last invincible enemy. That moment of clarity, power and knowledge is enough.'[7]

OUR PERSONAL MYTH:
A PLAY IN THREE ACTS

Our mindsets and automatic responses to given events can tend to impede our journey towards personal enlightenment, but what about all the people we have encountered in the course of our lives? Perhaps the healing process Dethlefsen and Dahlke refer to in their definition of the *Shadow* (*see* page 18) largely comes about through forgiveness, because two of our greatest obstacles to wholeness are guilt and shame. This is the universal theme in everyone's drama of life as set out in this three-act play – our own personal mythical story.

The preface to the drama of life is that most, if not all, of us feel obliged to attempt to make a gift to re-pay a debt we believe we owe to our parents, to society or even to the world at large.

Act I

In all good drama there must be conflict, the foundations of which are dictated by where we are born, which side of the tracks, status of family, colour, creed, nationality and so on. This sets up the drama that will unfold throughout the play, and Act I ends as soon as we leave home or get kicked out of the nest when we enter university, get a job, set up home, have relationships, get married, join the army, go to sea and begin to take responsibility for our selves.

Act II

Here we meet the good guys and the bad guys: those wearing the white hats are the people in our lives who love, nurture, bless, support and guide us. Those wearing black hats are the treacherous betrayers, the back-stabbers and those who let us down.

The white hats will not change us but simply maintain and sustain the status quo. It is only the black hats who will effect change – these are the people who teach us the lessons and experiences to move us on out of naivety.

As in all good drama, sometimes the good guys turn out to be bad guys and vice versa, bearing in mind that the underlying theme – the sub-text if you will – is that we are intent on making a 'gift'.

Act II does not end until we come to understand that all these people – both good and bad – are in our drama because it is we who have given them a role to play, so why should we be so upset when they are acting out perfectly what they were supposed to do? We set them up and chose them to be in our life drama. Therefore, we cannot blame them for their actions but accept that they are there for some good reason demanded by the *shadow*.

The only way we can get off this eternal, spinning and not so merry-go-round of Act II is to begin the process of *forgiveness*. This means forgiveness of mother, father, sister, brother and everyone else in our life, which ultimately means self-forgiveness. Only when we are released from the burden of blame, playing 'victim', and this meretricious obligation that we must make a gift will we be able to complete the play. Otherwise Act II will still be unfinished when we come to the end of this life.

Act III

Forgiveness releases the energy we have previously expended on blame and trying to make the 'gift'. It is only when self-forgiveness has released us from the burden of obligation that we can, if we so choose, freely make a true gift to humanity.

The drama which had all the makings of a tragedy thus ends and the comedy of life begins!

OUR JOURNEY ALONG THE TAROT'S PATHWAY

The following is a brief preview of the story of the mythical journey of the Hero/Heroine as told in the graphical, symbolic language of the Tarot. This journey along the Tarot's pathway is sometimes known as 'The 21 Steps to Freedom', and illustrations of the individual cards that correspond to its 21 steps will be found in plates 2–5.

Step One *(The Magician)*

Life is touched with magic and we are inspired to depart from the familiar to set out on a journey. Although we are naïve and immature neophytes or novices, at the back of our minds there is a faint understanding of an unbounded potential and the endless possibilities the good Earth and Heaven have given us.

Step Two *(The High Priestess)*

In our youth we sensed the presence of the invisible world of Spirit, but then we lost our connection to this invisible world. Now, however, we realize that there is more to life than the physical elements of earth, water, air and fire.

Steps Three and Four *(The Empress and The Emperor)*

At this point, we encounter and appreciate the Feminine Principles (intuition, the Mother Goddess, sex and sensuality) and the counterparts of the Masculine Principles (rationality, Father God, the earthy, earthly nature of the world about us, and material attainment). These two steps represent a 'marriage' between intuitive, instinctive thoughts and 'intellectual' thinking.

Step Five *(The Pope)*

The preceding two steps lead us to seek contact with a wise counsellor and other evolved people who will introduce us to a spiritual discipline and the divine knowledge of the sacred Cosmos.

Step Six *(The Lover)*

Here we need to form relationships, and by experiencing both the spiritual and philosophical worlds of mind and body we reach a major crossroads in our lives. Through love and relationships we are given a glimpse of what it would be like to be free from the fear of abandonment and to evolve a balance between our Masculine and Feminine Principles, thus becoming whole and complete. We can also become aware that our experiences so far may have served us, but have stifled the soul. We may have resented the demand to conform and resisted being disciplined in our thoughts and actions, and yet the inner voice urges us to accept the wise teachings and lessons from others to release the soul.

Step Seven *(The Chariot)*

We now stand at a crossroads. This is the critical moment when we must have the courage to let go of the reins and have complete trust and commitment in our quest. It is a journey into unknown, uncharted territory.

Step Eight *(Justice)*

This new beginning is marked by an acceptance of responsibility for our every thought and action and a willingness to maintain *balance* and discernment in all things.

Step Nine *(The Hermit)*

Here we walk between the material and spiritual worlds, seeking periods of solitude and contemplation to discover the self-sufficiency of our inner light.

Step Ten *(The Wheel of Fortune)*

This is popularly called *Karma,* otherwise known as the law of *Compensation.* Acceptance of responsibility for whatever cards 'lady luck' has dealt you implies that anybody and everybody whom you have ever met, befriended or had relationships with – including all those who have betrayed you or stabbed you in the back – have been drawn into your life by you! Even to the point that, as a soul, you chose your parents and the time to become a manifested being, because the characteristics, status, colour, creed and nationality of your parents offered you the tools, experiences, conflicts and attributes to enable you to move on to this current incarnation. The Wheel of Fortune is forever turning.

Step Eleven *(Force)*

This is the tipping point. We have journeyed this far but as yet remain unconscious of the mechanisms of our persona that control us. Now we must confront the 'stuff' of our early conditioning experiences – our inner demons and the fear of the unknown. Here, it would be so easy to succumb to the comforts of the ego, shy away from confrontation and live in ignorance of the *shadow.* But do we want to live the life of an unrealized person who has been captured and held in thrall by their complexes? In order to move on we must summon up all our resolve and inner strength.

Step Twelve *(The Hanged Man)*

This is the time to pause, reflect, take stock and gather our energies before venturing out of the apparent safety zone of illusionment and into the light. Again, courage is needed to review our values, accept reverses and prepare to be born again.

Step Thirteen *(Death)*

The idea of regeneration can fill us with fear and dread, but before we can be transformed – re-born – the 'old' self must die. Suddenly, and unbeknown to ourselves, we are on the path of initiation.

Steps Fourteen and Fifteen *(Temperance and The Devil)*

We now have a resurgence of energy that generates a sense of our innate potential and heaven-sent alchemical power. But this can be a dangerous moment when, perversely, we can easily retreat from our earlier resolve to become 'that which we already are' by suffering, fear and self-doubt. This is the Devil within us all.

Step Sixteen *(The Tower of Destruction)*

This step forward demands a sense of humility and a resolve to change our old ways of thinking and behaviour. Here we encounter a critical loss of direction, a breakdown in our ego consciousness and a crisis of identity.

Step Seventeen *(The Star)*

Here we pass on to an understanding of 'as above, so below' – the perennial view that what happens in the cosmos or the macroscopic realms is repeated in the microscopic world. With our new optimism and self-awareness, intuition comes to the fore. We become self-nurturing, we tread lightly over the Earth; we understand how to interact with the natural flow of life and become inspired by Nature and the Cosmos.

Step Eighteen *(The Moon)*

Heightened intuition and instinctive nature reinforce our relationship with the rhythms of the natural world, but we must beware of self-deception and illusions.

Step Nineteen *(The Sun)*

The path ahead is now clear. We have emerged out of the shadows and into the sunlight where we are open and as transparent to our selves as we are to others.

Step Twenty *(Judgement)*

Thus we can live by grace and enjoy being androgynous – to have a dynamic balance between the Masculine and Feminine principles personified by Sun and Moon. We no longer project our needs on to others or seek a 'crutch' from anyone. Instead we can give and receive love without conditions or wants. This is the release of the soul – a resurrection of the spirit (not the flesh) – and the realization that *spirit* is all around us. We are liberated from terrestrial limitations.

Step Twenty-One *(The World)*

Now the world is at our feet, we can dance with an inner joy and wisdom. We have fully realized the longings, wishful thinking and dreams of our naïve youthfulness; we are at one with ourselves and the universe; we are in a state of fulfilment and spiritual freedom.

We have healed our selves, discharged sorrow and have become integrated with the *Anima Mundi* – the World Soul. Our greatness is fulfilled, and now we must prepare to set out again to climb the next peak.

The Fool

The Fool encapsulates the whole process: at the beginning the Fool is confused, simple, naïve and indecisive. At the end the Fool becomes the Magus – a wise Fool who has grown in wisdom and knowledge with a sense of humanity. At the end of the journey we are still The Fool but no longer in a primordial state of naivety.

So far we have gained a broad idea about what the Tarot is telling us, but before we can 'read' the full import of the cards we must learn the language.

3

THE LANGUAGE OF THE TAROT

The powerful symbols of the Tarot are among the many emblems of those primordial images, by whose means the unchanging, universal aspects of reality may be apprehended.[1]

Imagine that you open your front door and standing on the threshold is a stranger who can only speak a language that is totally foreign and unknown to you. From the person's body language, facial expressions, gesticulations and tone of voice you can see that he or she is wanting to convey an important message to you, but you cannot understand what is being said.

Your first encounter with the Tarot can be like meeting that foreigner on your doorstep. In order to understand what the foreigner is saying, we need to learn their language. The same principle applies to the Tarot: before we can begin to understand what the Tarot is telling us, we first need to learn the conventions of its language. As our knowledge of the language increases, so will our understanding of the subtlety and import of what the Tarot is communicating to us.

The character images of the 22 Major Arcana cards and the Kings, Queens, Knights and Knaves in each of the four suits of the Minor Arcana cards will convey something to you through their body language, facial expressions, gestures, clothing and so on, in much the same manner that your intuition grasped a general impression of what the strange foreigner was trying to tell you: but the significance of these archetypal pictographs will be recognized and understood by our psyche as familiar characters we have encountered in fairy tales and our dreams.

Instinctively, we may get the vague feeling that important and profound messages are encoded in all the 78 cards of the Tarot. Intuitively, we begin to understand that the cards concern us: who we are, our foibles, desires, needs, our strivings for wholeness and fulfilment and the road we must travel to reach an unknown destination – wherever that may be. We may even find they offer us 'a glimpse into the infinite and eternal mystery of the one reality ... [and the] further layers of consciousness, which are universal in nature and extend beyond the layer of the collective unconscious into the universal sea of consciousness that we call Wisdom, the Divine Intelligence, the Universal Mind or the Mind of God.'[2]

Tarot is a language of pictographs and number symbols through which we can perceive transcendental wisdom. However, before we can comprehensively understand what the pictographs, suits and numbers mean, we must learn the *vocabulary* of that language. In his book *The Elements of Christian Symbolism*, John Baldock says that the importance, mystery and meaning of life, as expressed in myths and symbols ...

> ... lead us towards an infinite unity – and yet, as soon as
> we begin to analyse or define symbols as individual 'things'
> we start breaking that unity up into finite parts.
> Paradoxically, in exploring the possible meaning of a
> symbol we risk turning it into what is called a 'sign'.
>
> There is no mystery about the meaning of a sign. At its
> simplest level, for example a road sign, it is a practical,
> 'external' indicator that stands for, or informs us about, a
> known thing. On the other hand, a symbol is more the
> expression of something mysterious whose presence or
> existence, while still beyond the grasp of our rational
> mind, may be sensed in a way that is simultaneously
> 'internal' but distant. Through it our inner, unconscious or
> spiritual experience is united with our outer, sensory
> experience. As Father Sylvan in *Lost Christianity* expresses

it, 'The symbol is meant to guide the arising of the
unifying force within ourselves, the force which can bring
our aspects together, the force called "the Heart", the holy
desire.' To look at it more broadly, a symbol is an aid to
help us resolve the apparent diversity or multiplicity of
phenomenal things with the unity from which they
emanate.'[3]

In other words, a symbol such as an archetypal character or a number
represents something else by association, resemblance or convention
and expresses an inner dimension that has layers of meaning that are
understood more by the subconscious rather than the conscious mind.
In this regard, the language of the Tarot may be considered to be a
'sacred' language that employs an authentic and universally accepted
symbolism as often used in traditional myths and fairy tales.

Symbolism is the language of the Mysteries; in fact it is the
language not only of mysticism and philosophy but of all
Nature, for every law and power active in Universal
procedure is manifested to the limited sense perceptions of
Man through the medium of symbol...By symbols men
have ever sought to communicate to each other those
thoughts which transcend the limitations of
language...Mystics thus chose symbolism as a far more
ingenious and ideal method of preserving their transcendental knowledge. In a single figure a symbol may both
reveal and conceal, for to the wise the subject of the
symbol is obvious, while to the ignorant the figure remains
inscrutable.[4]

As we saw earlier, the basis of any language – including the Tarot – is
grammar, vocabulary and syntax. Grammar sets the rules governing
the relationship between words and their combinations. Vocabulary
relates to the meaning of words and the parts of speech and spelling.
Syntax is the grammatical arrangement of words and phrases.

All these are needed to form a rationality to create meaningful

patterns in order to communicate thoughts, feelings, ideas and philosophical or spiritual abstractions, and to ensure the intent is clearly
expressed. Unless there is a logical and organized structure there can be
no understanding or clear semantic comprehension of the language. The
language of the Tarot is complete in itself, representing distinct principles of human nature by means of the pictographs and numbers. All these
components are unique to the philosophy expressed in the cards.

Before embarking on an interpretation of individual cards and
their relevance within the deck as a whole, we first need to establish
a vocabulary of the symbolic language embodied in the pictographs
of the Major Arcana and the Minor Arcana Court cards as well as
the numbers of each card and the characteristics of each of the four
'suits'. This assumes that the motif of each pictograph and its
accompanying details – i.e. whether the figure is bearded or beardless, wearing a crown or hat, the colours of their clothing, their
accoutrements and so on – have a symbolic significance and contain
nothing superfluous nor any extraneous embellishments 'imported'
from other esoteric traditions. It also assumes that each number
and motif has a more or less universally accepted interpretation of
meaning and intent.

THE SYMBOLIC LANGUAGE
OF NUMBERS

The numbers One to Ten

Usually we think of numbers in terms of counting or measuring
quantities, but since ancient times the numbers one to ten have been
used as a qualitative symbolic language to express a paradigm or
model of the Universe.

Pythagoras (sixth century BCE), the Greek philosopher, spiritual
leader and mystic who revealed the esoteric meanings of mathematics, geometry and music, said, 'evolution is the Law of Life, number is
the Law of the Universe; unity is the Law of God.' He believed that

everything in the Universe was subject to predictable, progressive cycles measured by the numbers one to nine and each number symbolized a specific archetypal characteristic. For example, the number five 'represents that particular "playful" aspect of the One Reality by which the human microcosm, or "little universe" reflects the perfect order of the macrocosm or "greater universe". As part of that particular play we have the capacity to contemplate the perfection of the universe for ourselves, through our five senses.'[5]

The early Greek philosophers defined the number of Nature (the Cosmos) as the *Decad*. They also expressed the enigma of *the Creation* with the riddle 'ten is complete at four', which can be interpreted as meaning that the cosmic creative process has four stages expressed symbolically through the numbers one (unity), two (duality), three (trinity or reconciliation) and four (the manifested, material world) which together $(1 + 2 + 3 + 4 = 10)$ represent *the whole of Creation*. It can therefore be said that ten (the Cosmos) completes itself at four (the manifestation of the material world). Through the first principle and abstract language of mathematics and *numbers* we can begin to comprehend and understand the Cosmos.

This squares with St Augustine's view that 'numbers are the thoughts of God. ... The Divine Wisdom is reflected in the numbers impressed on all things ... [and] the construction of the physical and moral world alike is based on eternal numbers.'[6]

Numbers were metaphors expressing the ancient concept that there is unity in all existence, in everything that is tangible, in everything we can sense and even in our patterns of thought.

Whilst the symbolic conventions of the examples given below attribute a degree of variation to the meanings of the numbers, each system more or less conforms to interpretations universally accepted as being integral to sacred teachings.

A Platonic System for the Numbers One to Ten

The Platonic 'convention' for the symbolism of the numbers one to ten is as follows:

1 The unity of all things; the beginning of creation; God and the Divine Spirit.

2 Duality; the separation into masculine and feminine (Adam and Eve).

3 The trinity; the reconciliation, the return to wholeness and the dynamic symmetry of mind, body and spirit.

4 The manifested, material world of matter represented by the four elements of fire, earth, air and water.

5 The product of two (the first prime even number, representing the female principle) plus three (the first odd prime number, representing the male principle). Five symbolizes Mankind, human love, harmony and health, the five senses and the four elements + ether – the *quintessence*. The five pointed star – the pentacle – is recognized as the sigil of Mankind.

6 The divine harmony of the child – creativity – resulting from the marriage or integration of the masculine and feminine principles (2 + 3 + 1).

7 Seven measures the changing seasons, the rhythm of life and the Cosmos; the Moon cycles; the seven colours of the rainbow; the seven power centres (chakras) of the body; and the seven days of the week. Plato's Seven Liberal Arts were, and still are, the foundation of the teachings of the ancient Mystery Schools.

8 The octave linking Heaven and Earth (as above, so below). Eight represents new beginnings; the start of a new cycle and raised energies.

9 Absolute passivity; detachment and human frailty; the need to pause before completion.

10 The Decad – representing the whole creation.

A Renaissance System for the Numbers One to Nine

Some readers may find resonance with Agrippa of Nettesheim (1486–1555), the Renaissance philosopher/alchemist, and his interpretation of the symbolic significance of the numbers one to nine:

1 Action; ambition; leadership.
2 Balance; passivity; receptivity.
3 Gaiety; versatility; ebullience.
4 Endurance; steadiness; dullness.
5 Sexuality; adventure; instability.
6 Domesticity; harmony; dependability.
7 Mystery; knowledge; solitariness.
8 Worldly involvement coupled with material success.
9 Spirituality; inspiration and great achievement.[7]

It is interesting to note that the number nine has unusual qualities: if nine is added to any other number – high or low – it will not change the sum of the digits. For example, the sum of 17 (1 + 7) = 8; add 9 = 17. Or again, 92 (9 + 2) = 11, which is then reduced to 2 (1 + 1); add 9 = 11 and so on.[8] There is a correspondence here between this 'unchanging' quality of the number nine with the ninth card of the Major Arcana, The Hermit, which represents the unchanging core of our being (*see* page 67).

A Hermetic System

Hermes, known as Hermes Trismegistus (Hermes the Thrice-Great-One), is said to be the combined reincarnation of Moses and the Egyptian god Thoth. One of the great philosophers alongside Socrates and Plato, Hermes revealed to Mankind medicine, chemistry (alchemy), magic, law, astrology, geometry, music, anatomy, oratory and blends of mysticism and natural science. The Emerald Tablet (otherwise known as the *Tabula Smaragdina*), the oldest and most revered of all alchemical formulae, is ascribed to Hermes. The *Hermetic Laws* provide another variation on number symbolism:

- The law of Polarity – Adversarial combat (number two)
- The law of Resonance – Harmony (number three)
- The law of Manifestation – The four elements (number four)
- The law of Correspondence – As above, so below (number eight).
- The law of Compensation – sometimes known as Karma (number ten)

The Numbers Eleven to Twenty-Two

JE Cirlot suggests that as all the numbers beyond ten are produced by either adding or multiplying the digits in the first numbers 1 to 10, a possible meaning of the numbers 11 to 21 may be deduced by taking the example of number 21: the left-hand digit (2) symbolizes, say, separation or conflict and (1) stands for unity or the unifying process. This suggests that the outcome of a situation denoted by the left-hand digit is resolved by the right-hand digit.[9] In particular, three other significant numbers used in occult traditions are 11, 19 and 22.

Number 11

Number 11 is the product of 1 (God) plus 10 (completion).

Because it is one in excess of perfection it could denote humankind trying to go beyond 'God' or the natural world. It is associated with revelation and enlightenment and signifies the completion of all Karmic causation and the conclusion of our Earthly work.

However, there is a consensus of opinion that the number also represents the Mandorla which has the shape of an almond and the geometry of the Vesica Piscis. It is also the symbol of the Yoni or female genitals, often referred to in both exoteric (erotic) and esoteric circles as the 'gateway to heaven'.

The eleventh card (Force) in the Major Arcana is in the significant central position and marks a critical turning point.

Number 12

The integration of spirit (3) multiplied by the 4 elements suggests cosmic order, time and space, and the 12 days to bring order out of chaos. Number 12 implies a separation from 'god' or being in a state of suspension from the world of Spirit.

Number 13

Since 1 is unity and 3 represents mind, body and spirit, number 13 is about a return to the source – a death and re-birth. Or 1 + 3 equals the four elements with connotations of 'ashes to ashes' and 'dust to dust', but this is a symbolic *death* and heralds a psychological/spiritual change rather than a physical demise.

Number 14

This is Cosmic Order imposed upon the four elements.

Number 15

This can denote spiritual regression caused by human frailty (5) leading to excessive hedonism or eroticism.

Number 16

The numbers 1 + 6 represent the end of another octave and the beginning of something new in our attitude to life and living. It suggests we might use our creativity and energies for higher purposes.

Number 17

The numbers 1 + 7 represent heaven and earth and worldly endeavour tempered by the spirit.

Number 18

This again is our spiritual essence (1) tempered by our heaven-sent gifts and natural instincts and intuition.

Number 19

The numbers 1 + 9 return us to 10 but with a greater depth of under-standing of ourselves as spiritual, as well as temporal, beings. The addition of numbers 10 and 9 represents 'Divine order and judgment'.

The sacred texts of the Bible – Ezekiel, Ezra, Enoch – and other holy books such as the Koran were written in a secret code using let-ters/numbers as ciphers to conceal their mystical knowledge so that the profound teachings would be available only to those initiates who had been taught how to decode the numbers. This system of writing arcane texts is known as *Gematria*. Scholars have shown that the numerous times the number 19 is encoded in a word or sequence of words in the texts of both the Bible and the Koran is beyond coincidence.

The source of esoteric teachings and ancient wisdom can often be traced to Cosmic events and the order of the universe. It is therefore not surprising that the natural cycles of the Sun and Moon meet every 19 years, and that every 19 years we witness a full eclipse of the Sun. In the Major Arcana of the Tarot, the nineteenth card is The Sun.

Number 20

Zero, associated with The Fool, has unmanifested, infinite potential and, like the seed, has the whole of life encoded in an apparently inert being. Twenty concerns unexpected creativity (2) that has become manifested. It can also represent the complete Man/Woman.

Number 21

Separation and duality (2) have become resolved by the spirit of unity (1). The numbers 1 + 2 represent wholeness, fulfilment and the inte-gration of mind, body and spirit as a completely realized, self-expressed person. Twenty-one represents World Order – God and the Cosmos.

Number 22

As we shall see in chapter 4, the Major Arcana cards are numbered 1 to 21, whilst the twenty-second card – The Fool – is unnumbered or zero because, being the *Joker* in the pack it can manifest anywhere at any time in our daily life. The number 22 marks the entry into the light of eternal life and can represent The Fool as a fully-realized being.

The number 22 is also the unit measure of the circumference of a circle when the diameter is 7: (22 divided by $7 = \pi$) which is a fraction that goes on to infinity without ever producing a whole number.

Number 22 reflects the Kabbalistic tenet that God spoke in a sacred language using the 22 characters of the Hebraic alphabet

THE SYMBOLISM OF THE
PICTOGRAPHS

The following glossary provides the reader with the conventional interpretation of the symbols associated with the cards of the Major Arcana. The Court cards of the Minor Arcana employ the same symbolic vocabulary, but for the sake of clarity they have been omitted from the bracketed notes and are dealt with later in chapter 5.

Animals

Animals represent the instinctive and psychic energy of the natural world.

Horse   Forces of life, freedom of spirit (The Chariot)

Monkey   Mischieviousness (The Wheel of Fortune)

Dog   Protection (The Fool, The Moon)

Eagle   All-seeing, high-flying noble creature (an emblem on the shields of The Empress and The Emperor, and pictured in The World; see also Sulphur)

Lion   King of the forest, courage, territorially ferocious (Force, The World)

Scorpion/ **Lobster**	This crustaceous creature lives in the deep waters and protects its soft inner body with a hard outer shell (The Moon)
Fish	The life force in the waters of chaos (The Moon)
Bull	Thoughtfulness, placid nature (The World)

Colours

The laurel wreath framing The World's dancer is made up of the three primary colours – red, blue, yellow – from which all other colours, tones and shades derive. It is the combination to produce infinite creativity. The wreath of laurels also indicates 'success'.

Blue	Emotion, feminine intuition, feelings, sensitivity, healing, creativity, religion
Green	Fertility, growth, tangible earthiness, Nature, adaptability
Gold	Illumination, alchemical transformation, salvation, eternal life, immortality. Gold never dims. It is also the colour of Sulphur
Red	Rationality, life blood, sexual energy, power, vitality, fire, passion, life-giving
Pink	Sensuality, colour of flesh, sensitivity, resurrection
Yellow	Intellect/'gut feelings', Sun, Cosmos, light
White	Transformation (The Magician's knife, the Cupid's bow and arrow in The Lover's, the collar of the charioteer in The Chariot, the sword in The Wheel Of Fortune,

The Hanged Man's tunic and knot, Temperance's elixir, The Devil's weapon, The Fool's stick)

Black   Death and transformation (Death, The Devil, The Star's bird)

Columns

A single column represents the World Axis – *Axis Mundi* – and the phallic symbol of fertility and ego, pride (The Tower of Destruction).

Twin columns can represent Divine Man and Earthly Man and the opposing forces that create eternal stability: eagerness and strength, action and passivity, mercy and severity, good and bad, light and darkness, birth and death (The Pope, Justice, The Hanged Man, The Moon).

The four columns supporting the canopy over the Charioteer may represent the four rivers of paradise.

Crowns

A crown denotes spiritual or temporal 'royalty' – a status that indicates the acquisition of knowledge, understanding, wisdom and spiritual insights. The jewels in the crown are not to display wealth but each precious stone has a specific vibrational property that enhances the wearer's psychic / spiritual qualities.

The High Priestess and The Pope have elaborate triple crowns suggesting power over the three worlds – the material, psychological and spiritual realms.

The Emperor's crown is large and elaborate, signifying the extent of his domain and power.

The Charioteer's small crown suggests 'he is getting there'.

Justice wears an oversized crown with one golden 'jewel'.

The monkey on The Wheel of Fortune has a relatively simple crown design.

The crowns denote various levels of initiation: the largest crown – our ego – is toppled in The Tower of Destruction.

Feet

Feet represent our lower or earthly / earthy nature.

Bare feet indicate a sense of humanity, an expression of humbleness or humility, a renunciation of earthly, material things (The Emperor, The Lover, Death, The Devil, The Star, The Sun, The World).

Hair

Golden hair or ringlets suggest a youthful, everlasting quality or potential, and immortality (The Magician).

Flesh-coloured hair denotes sensitivity about human nature (Justice, The Hermit, Force, The Sun, The World).

Blue hair suggests intuitive insight, a quality associated with the feminine principle (The Pope, The Hanged Man, Temperance, The Tower Of Destruction, The Star, The Moon, Judgement).

Long thick hair on a male figure – such as a god, a hero or a man – indicates virility, vitality and power. (Samson's phallic power resided in his hair. It was cut off by Delilah to 'castrate' him and draw his energy into herself.)

A woman's long, unbound hair was attributed to her psychic, magical, spiritual powers, hence women accused of witchcraft had their hair shaved. Throughout history to the present day, men's suppression of the feminine psychic powers has demanded women to have their head covered. (The hair of Medusa – the terrible Gorgon whose look turned men to stone – was a nest of serpents.)

The High Priestess voluntarily covers her hair to announce that she has forsaken her psychic witch-like powers and suppresses sexual attraction.

White hair suggests the quality of transformation (The Empress, The Emperor, The Pope).

Having no hair indicates an absence of psychic or any other powers (Death).

A beard represents masculine wisdom (The Emperor, The Pope, The Hermit).

Beardlessness indicates masculinity, youthfulness, immaturity, innocence and naivety (The Magician, The Lover, The Chariot, The Hanged Man, The Devil, The Tower Of Destruction, The Sun).

(Note: The Fool has the semblance of a beard indicating he can be either a person of wisdom or naivety.)

Headgear

Whereas a crown indicates status, a hat suggests who we are, our motives and where we are going in our daily life.

The Magician's hat is shaped like the sign of infinity (a lemniscate or ribbon of unbounded potentiality), fertile, energized and golden. This sigil is repeated in the hat worn by Force.

Temperance wears a red rose in her hair – a flower of love.

The Devil's headgear is chaotic and golden; the two figures are naked except for red and black head-dresses.

The World's dancer is adorned with a flesh-coloured scarf.

The Fool wears a strange golden hat with a red bauble that covers his head and neck.

Mode of Direction

The Fool, The Pope, Force, Death are orientated or moving towards their left which expresses a tendency towards psychological/spiritual transformation

The characters looking towards the right – The Magician, The High Priestess, the Lover the Chariot and The Hermit – are either involved or in the process of becoming involved in the discovery of their inner world. The other group – Temperance, The Star, The Moon and the World – also oriented towards their right has discovered and live by their inner world and intuition

The Empress looking to her left and the Emperor, looking to his right indicate the contrasting modes of intuition and rationality in the day-by-day temporal world.

The characters looking straight ahead – The Hanged Man and The Devil – are in a state of static inertia whereas Justice, The Sun and the herald in Judgement indicate an unconditional, dynamic balance.

Ribbons

A streamer of magical force and energy represented by the figure of eight '∞' – the lemniscate (The Magician, Force, The World).

Rod, Staff or Wand

The wand represents a magical rod of power when held in the left hand (The Magician, The World).

The Fool also has a rod or stick in his left hand and a staff in his right: both act as 'weapons' to protect him on his journey.

The Hermit holds a crooked staff in his left hand to denote that he takes an intuitive (indirect) route to arrive at his journey's destination.

Similarly, The Pope holds a staff with a triple cross in his gloved left hand.

There are semblances of a staff – or are they swords? – held in the left hand of the monkey in The Wheel of Fortune and of The Devil, suggesting a sinister connotation.

Rope

The Devil's rope indicates that the characters are tied to existence in a material world.

The knot restraining The Hanged Man is the umbilical cord that needs to be cut to release him from his conditioning.

Sceptre and Orb

The sceptre and orb carried by The Empress (left hand) and The Emperor (right hand) denote their legal power. The sceptre is the male phallic symbol of virility, the orb is the Earth, and together they express the fertile sexual relationship between a king and queen. The cross on the orb suggests that the union is blessed by a spiritual power and links heaven and earth.

The Charioteer in The Chariot is holding a sceptre and orb in his right hand but it is a lightweight instrument without the symbol of spiritual dominance.

Sulphur

Sulphur (represented by the letter 'S' in chemistry) is a yellow non-toxic solid element also known as brimstone – the fires of hell and devils. In alchemy it is supposed to be one of the ultimate elements of all material substances – the other two are salt and mercury. It is associated with the Sun and can symbolize the eagle. (*See* 'Yellow' on page 40.) We must bear in mind that the formulae and emblems of alchemy are allegorical, metaphoric symbols and not to be interpreted in a literal sense.

Throne

Symbol of power both temporal and spiritual (The High Priestess, The Empress, The Emperor, The Pope, Justice).

Tower

The tower represents a spiritual connection between heaven and earth and the strength of the human spirit. The tower of Babel symbolized pride, ego and self-destruction. A watchtower had windows that allowed light to penetrate the inner darkness and the three windows in The Tower Of Destruction may represent a pair of eyes and the 'third eye'.

Water

The chaotic primordial waters of the deep; the ever-flowing source of life; an expression of the full spectrum of emotions and perpetual creation. Droplets of water come from the ocean and return to it, representing transformation and enlightenment (The Star, The Moon).

TO SUMMARIZE

The language of symbols is not exclusive to myths and fairy tales; in our everyday life we can recognize many of the symbol conventions set out above. We can see them in the ceremonial establishments of royalty, the judiciary and Parliament with their crowns, wigs, cardinal hats, orbs and sceptres, swords and ermine capes; we speak of 'green issues' which imply matters of the heart rather than of logic or the head. Those familiar with the Hindu Chakra system will recognize the colours attributed to the power centres in the body and the vibrational frequencies of light. Animals express national or personal characteristics – the bulldog, the cockerel, the lion and so on – and symbolic images are used in all the visual arts.

This chapter is a broad guide to help the reader and student to interpret aspects of the pictorial symbolism and number metaphors used in both the Major and the Minor cards. As we become more familiar with the pack we will recognize the combination of the symbols in the pictographs and numbers of each card and go further to discover how the cards are related to each other as if we were reading a story book. We will also tend to develop our own selective and usually condensed interpretations of the symbols to facilitate our own unique 'shorthand' comprehension of the knowledge and wisdom of the Tarot.

The next two chapters are an attempt – essays if you will – to use the above vocabulary, lexicon or glossary of terms to bring a depth of *meaning* to the language of the Tarot. In other words, it deals with *syntax* – 'The way in which words are put together grammatically to form phrases and sentences,'[10] 'or an orderly or systematic arrangement of parts or elements; a connected order or system of things.'[11]

DECODING THE
MAJOR ARCANA

This chapter is a guide to draw the reader's attention to the detail in the illustrations with suggested commentary and interpretations of the symbolism. These suggestions, which are based on the actual information expressed in each pictograph and sequence of numbering, are not intended to be the one and only *definitive* set of interpretations: it is up to the individual to study and read into the cards whatever may be meaningful for them. Inevitably, there will be personal preferences and diverse variations that will arise when deciphering or 'reading' the cards in a spread.

The cards of the Major Arcana represent the 21 steps we can take on the path to self-knowledge and spiritual transformation – from The Magician (I) to The World (XXI) – plus a twenty-second, unnumbered card: The Fool. (The designers of some modern Tarot decks have rearranged the Major Arcana cards in a different sequence, while others have omitted numbering them altogether to suit their own interpretation of the Tarot.)

In the previous chapter we explored a broad interpretation of the symbolism attributed to the numbers 1 to 22. At this stage it is only natural to ask whether this symbolism also applies to the Roman numerals on each of the 21 cards of the Major Arcana, or do their numerals simply indicate the sequence of the 21 milestones or steps that mark the path to self-knowledge? The answer to this question will become apparent in later chapters when we explore the cards of the Minor Arcana. In the present chapter, the description of each of the 22 pictographs of the Major Arcana includes an explanation of the symbolic significance of the actual number of each card based on the symbolism set out in the previous chapter. The cards of the Major Arcana are illustrated in full colour in the plate section.

The Fool

The 22nd card The Fool, sometimes known as *The Joker*, is unnumbered. It can either be thought of as zero – meaning 'unmanifested' – or interpreted as number 22, meaning 'entry into eternal life' or as *pi* (π) representing infinity. (*See* plate 1.)

The Fool is 'within' each one of the other 21 Major Arcana cards and inevitably will appear and influence our progress at any point along the path.

Figure 1: The Fool

The Fool is a male figure personifying both the Masculine and the Feminine Principles in both men and women. His face could be that of a mature man, or perhaps the semblance of a 'designer-style' beard suggests a more youthful character. Maybe the protruding jaw represents his manner of 'sticking his chin out' – one of the traits of a naïve person. The elaborate headgear with its red bauble expresses an eccentricity, or it may conceal an abundance of hair to suggest that – like other pilgrims – his hair is left uncut until he returns home. He is on a journey, travelling to his left.

The neckpiece of bells, his tunic, girdle and a pair of blue hose or cloth leggings, usually worn by working people, are similar to those worn by late-14th-century court jesters. A dog bites the back of his leg, ripping his hose and exposing his right upper thigh. In his left hand, but over his right shoulder, he is carrying a bag of his worldly possessions and sustenance. The white stick suggests he may be searching for transformation from the burden of carrying his material goods and the golden staff in his right hand is intended to protect and help him on his way along the fertile but difficult and uneven terrain.

His gaze skyward suggests he may be day-dreaming. Certainly he is unaware of the dog (instinctual protection) attacking him from behind (his unconsciousness) trying to draw his attention from where he is heading.

The Fool is unnumbered: it can be zero, which ineffably encompasses everything; it can be the 22nd card (22 is the ancient number for a circle – the circle of life) or it can be neither or both. He is in no one place but is present in each of the 21 numbered cards like anti-matter in quantum physics. We are like The Fool: pathetic in our struggle to reach a higher level of consciousness. He personifies every phase of our life from being naïve and arrogant, carrying the heavy baggage of our worldly goods and psychological conditioning, to becoming an evolved, transformed person of wisdom who lives by grace and one who has learned to be a 'man/woman of knowledge'.

The Fool may be a precocious, foolish, immature character who, like Peter Pan – the *Puer Aeternus* – is full of youthful vigour and only wants to play games. In this mode he is mischievous, capricious, idealistic, lacking discipline and is often an unreliable lover. These negative aspects may be summed up by Robert Bly's definition of a naïve person:

- Believes everyone is honest, sincere, straightforward and speaks from the heart
- Will lose what is most precious because he or she knows no boundaries
- Will confide last night's special dream to a stranger
- Has special relationships but never examines or recognizes their *shadow*
- Picks up the pain of others and is attracted to other people who share their pain (Listening to people's pain is compassionate, but sharing pain is a negative indulgence because there is no need or benefit to carry other people's pain.)
- Lacks a natural compassionate ruthlessness (won't kick children out of the nest)
- Will not agree to follow instructions but also won't admit that he or she is ignoring the instructions – whatever they may be
- The timing is always off
- Acts out self-enforced periods of isolation
- Sinks into moods of deep depression
- Wants to remain sick
- Feels pride in being attacked and 'bares his chest' (or sticks out his chin) for more[1].

As we saw in the three-act play (*see* page 21), naivety invites betrayal – this is the psyche at work, setting up attractive people and situations until the relevant lessons are learned.

However, The Fool can represent perception, developed intuition, versatility and wisdom – one who can act the fool light-heartedly without being foolish or foolhardy. The Fool can have all the attributes of Castaneda's 'Man of Knowledge' as well as being able to turn the conventional world upside down as we do on April Fool's Day. In medieval courts the fool, jester or clown was the king's alter ego and the only person the king or queen could turn to for an honest opinion without taking offence. His youthful, child-like 'clowning about' could hide from others a deeper understanding of whatever issues were at hand.

The Fool represents aspects of each one of us as the Hero or Heroine on our journey through life. The card is the 'joker' in the pack and, as we shall see later, its significance is dependent upon where it appears in a spread and the other cards around it, which will indicate either naivety or maturity. This card flags up a warning that something is not exactly as it may appear to be – i.e. we need to pause before taking action – or it may herald a quirk of fate with unexpected twists and turns that may inspire us to change our way of thinking or even enjoy the unexpected outcome! When we dwell in darkness and confusion, it is through The Fool that we can emerge from the *shadow* and progress from illusion to self-realization.

THE MAJOR ARCANA CARDS

The 21 cards from The Magician to The World can best be read as three segments of seven cards each (*see* plate 2).

The first group of seven cards on our journey of initiation begins with The Magician and ends with The Chariot. They represent the process of learning and overcoming the fear of stepping into unknown territory.

The second group begins with Justice and ends with Temperance. These are the steps that lead to clarity of mind.

The third group, from The Devil to The World, is the final and the most demanding sector of the journey. Here we encounter The Devil and The Tower of Destruction to warn of the dangers of believing that our newly acquired clarity of mind and sense of feeling invincible may induce a temptation to misuse the power. If we do not succumb to these fateful hazards, we can proceed to complete the heroic journey to freedom and self-knowledge.

Ancien Tarot de Marseille

THE FOOL

Plate 1

Plate 2

Plate 3

Plate 4

Plate 5

Plate 6

Plate 7

Plate 8

Plate 9

Plate 10

Plate 11

Plate 12

Plate 13

Plate 14

Plate 15

Plate 16

Plate 17

Plate 18

Plate 19

Plate 20

Plate 21

Plate 22

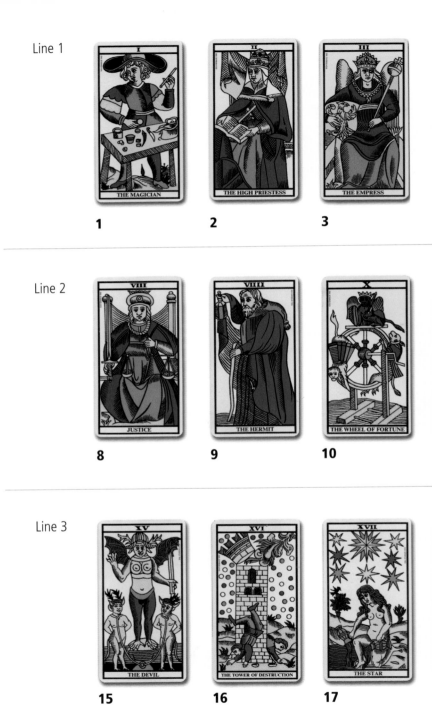

Line 1

1 THE MAGICIAN 2 THE HIGH PRIESTESS 3 THE EMPRESS

Line 2

8 JUSTICE 9 THE HERMIT 10 THE WHEEL OF FORTUNE

Line 3

15 THE DEVIL 16 THE TOWER OF DESTRUCTION 17 THE STAR

Plate 23. **The Major Arcana 21-Card Spread**

4

5

6

7

11

12

13

14

18

19

20

21

Examples of the Numbered Cards

Plate 24: **4 of Money**

Plate 25: **5 of Cups**

Plate 26: **7 of Swords**

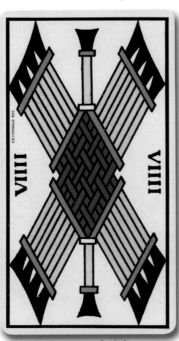

Plate 27: **9 of Clubs**

The Court Cards of Money

Plate 28

Plate 29

Plate 30

Plate 31

The Court Cards of Cups

THE KNAVE OF CUPS

Plate 32

THE KNIGHT OF CUPS

Plate 33

THE QUEEN OF CUPS

Plate 34

THE KING OF CUPS

Plate 35

The Court Cards of Swords

Plate 36

Plate 37

Plate 38

Plate 39

The Court Cards of Clubs

Plate 40

Plate 41

Plate 42

Plate 43

I The Magician

The Magician is a beardless youth with white hair and golden ringlets. The dominant, overlarge hat, similar to the Italian style of the period, is in the shape of the lemniscate or curve of ribbons and is reminiscent of the figure of eight on its side, the mathematical sign for infinity or completeness.

According to Barbara Walker, the lemniscate is composed of a clockwise (male, solar) circle and an anti-clockwise (female, lunar) circle and represents the two becoming one – a universal theme that is also expressed through the Taoist symbol for Yin and Yang.[2]

The choice of an eccentric, motley, multi-coloured tunic and hose – even his shoes don't match – expresses his uniqueness that marks him out from the crowd. It also suggests opposing energies. There is a

Figure 2: I. The Magician

resemblance to The Fool's tunic and gold belt. The Magician's downward gaze to his right suggests that he is less concerned with the worldly accoutrements laid out on the table than with his inner world. His left hand tentatively holds a wand (a magic rod of power and intuition) and in his right hand, held by his fingertips, he has a gold coin representing the material world. Although his feet are planted firmly on the fertile ground, they are pointing in different directions.

The three-legged table looks decidedly too unstable to support the objects of gold coins, a cup, a knife, a blue feather, some dice and a bag (of tricks?) which may represent the five elements and 'the luck of the dice'. All these, including his magic wand of creative intelligence, inspiration and imagination, are the essential 'tools' he will need on life's journey. He is still an uninitiated neophyte but has the infinite potential to use the gifts at his disposal to integrate his innate spirituality with his material earthiness. Used wisely, these gifts will enable him to discover and develop the necessary self-awareness to become a complete and fully realized person: otherwise the naïve Fool will prevail and he will remain the little boy – the *Puer Aeternus*.

In our daily lives we can meet real magicians in their many guises: they might be a sorcerer, a confidence trickster, a manipulator, a 'creative accountant', a seducer and juggler of money and emotions. In their positive mode, he or she could be an analyst, a researcher, creative inventor, a writer, thinker and planner, 'Q' in the James Bond films, the Enigma code-breakers. These people are the 'back-room boys and girls' who prefer to work behind the scenes rather than be in the limelight.

The Magician is the trickster who needs to understand and come to terms with his *shadow* to control the temptation to misuse his innate talents and power. His story (our story) begins with a departure from a familiar and comfortable way of life in order to meet strangers and travel along unfamiliar pathways.

Although he is a young person, he has infinite potential. As card number I, he embodies the Divine Spirit present within us all.

II The High Priestess

Her hair, the symbol of female psychic and sexual power, is concealed under a white wimple headdress. The jewelled ecclesiastical triple crown signifies her spiritual status and intellectual prowess. She is gazing straight ahead to her right because she knows by heart the contents of the book of spiritual laws that hold the keys to secret doctrines.

Her voluminous, flowing blue mantle (healing and emotional strength), with its gold collar and neckpiece and the gold fastening across her breast, are in the traditional Norman fashion of the 13th century. The mantle covers her red cotte (spiritual fire energy) and flesh-coloured kirtle.

Figure 3: II The High Priestess

Partly hidden under the mantle is a gold wand, indicating her magical rod of occult power. With the exception of her hands and gently smiling face, her body is completely concealed under the costume and, as we cannot detect her feet, we can only surmise that she is not earth-bound. She sits comfortably on her throne and behind her head is a veil or curtain that protects the secrets of divine wisdom from the uninitiated. Here, the neophyte is committed to follow a path that leads to the first encounter with spiritual discipline and feminine wisdom.

This card number II symbolizes the Feminine Principle and duality. The High Priestess personifies both virginity (innocence) and the wise old crone (spirituality), but it also implies the separation and isolation of the independent woman who, like Persephone, dwells in the underworld but re-emerges with the coming of Spring and then descends again in the Winter.

III The Empress

Like The High Priestess, The Empress also wears an elaborate, temporal jewelled crown that sits easily on her head, but her white hair expresses her overt sexuality and flowing transformation. She too is gazing ahead, but half towards her left. The blue cotte is pulled up to show her red kirtle and, like women of high rank of the period, the waist is ungirdled to leave the dress long and flowing.

The heavily ornamented gold collar and girdle beneath her breast mark her as a royal person possessing material wealth. This is reinforced by the shield emblazoned with an eagle (spirit within matter, and the protective, all-seeing eye) facing in the same direction and held in her right hand. In her left hand she lightly carries a golden orb (Mother Earth) and sceptre (phallic rod of power). The cross and band on the sceptre link Heaven with Earth and the marriage of masculine and feminine – the king and queen.

Although her concealed feet may not be completely on the ground, the outline of her open thighs suggest the full range of Aphrodite's attributes: sensuality, erotic love, compassion, harmony, beauty, fertility

Figure 4: III The Empress

and abundance. Her comfortable and open posture on the well-uphol-stered throne might imply that she is receptive to sexual advances.

The Empress personifies the tangible World; the collective consciousness; our relationship of body and spirit and the creative feminine forces. In her negative mode she can become over-emotional, possessive, overbearingly dominant and stifle the creativity in others. If she is 'a little girl' she will want to keep her sons as little boys and not allow their independence. When she is a benevolent Mother Goddess she can stimulate, heal, encourage versatility and vitality and, as with all fertile women, she experiences cyclical changes and variable seasons.

Here the neophyte experiences the full-blooded range of The Empress's anima principle (intuition) and the world of the senses and the tangible universe. Number III is about creating resolutions through mediation and compassion.

IIII The Emperor

The ornate, almost too-heavy-to-wear crown suggests he carries weighty responsibilities and has supreme authority. His full white beard and tresses are the mark of a mature man who is not necessarily wise but one who rules by reason and intellect. He is fully turned to his right, looking ahead. The white shoes, his crossed leg and his stance, balanced only on one foot, could indicate that although he has great wealth and power, he treads lightly on the earth. He is perched rather than sitting firmly on an elaborately carved throne, which is fitted with well-padded upholstery and devoid of concealing drapery. Although relaxed, he is poised ready to take action. His crossed legs form the shape of a letter 'S' – the symbol for sulphur (*see* Yellow, page 40, and Sulphur, page 45).

Figure 5: IIII The Emperor

The elaborate gold chain and jewel pendant (the burden of responsibility) also marks his royal status. The blue tunic and hose with a red cope (a hooded cloak) indicate that his principal mode of thinking and action is controlled by a passionate rationality rather than emotional considerations, while the golden girdle grasped in his left hand suggests that he trusts his earthy 'gut' feelings.

In contrast to The Empress, his right hand carries a heavier weight of orb and sceptre held in an upright position; his shield is also more elaborately decorated and the eagle faces the same direction as him. Again, unlike The Empress, he has no need to hold on to or carry the shield's symbol of power: he knows he can use it whenever he chooses. The eagle's claws span over the golden fertile earth.

The Emperor is the father figure – the animus – and both he and The Empress rule over the same realm. He exudes the virility and self-assertion of a powerful king and lawmaker who relies on rationality and strength of intellect. Number IIII personifies materiality and the material world.

A king can be a benevolent leader who blesses and encourages rather than offering nothing but criticism; he will be a protector who understands limitations and acts wisely. Alternatively, he can rule like a tyrant or weakling, with no sense of boundaries or justice, whose unrealistic ambitions can lead to failure or loss.

When the neophyte meets The Emperor, he or she confronts authority, order, the rules of self-discipline and behaviour, which will threaten any childish behaviour. Any traces of pride, frustration, rebelliousness and selfishness would hinder or even completely block further progress along the path.

V The Pope

The bejewelled triple crown expresses power over the three worlds – the exoteric, mesoteric and esoteric realms – and a rich knowledge and mastery of the mysteries of life. His white flowing hair and full beard signify maturity and wisdom, which are similar to The Emperor's but reflect a spiritual rather than a temporal or Earthly plane of

Figure 6: V The Pope

existence. (An abundance of hair and beard marked out a person who had been on a pilgrimage.) The red cope edged in gold, fastened with a mors – an ecclesiastical jewelled fastening – covers the voluminous blue robe that envelops the whole of his body. The sleeves of his undergarment are white: his right hand is blessing his congregation, and in his gloved left hand (concealing an iron fist?) he holds a triple cross to reinforce the threefold symbolism of the crown.

The throne raises him above the exoteric, material plane. It has two blue phallic symbols that may refer to the two pillars representing firmness and strength in the Temple of Solomon, the wise ruler.

Kneeling at his feet are four students or disciples (are they the four elements?) wearing copes and rolled cloth hats suggesting their humble status, but the hole in the centre of the headpiece – similar to the shaved tonsure of monks – indicates they are receptive to The Pope's wisdom and enlightenment which penetrates the skull to the pineal gland. The Pope is a 'king' of orthodox spiritual doctrine; a teacher, and one who can reveal to us the unknown that bridges the gap between Heaven and Earth. He offers the opportunity to transform purely material desires into loving generosity; to overcome physical needs and thus avoid compulsive attachments, and how to set aside an extravagant, obsessive lifestyle in exchange for balanced simplicity.

The four archetypes – teachers if you will – The High Priestess, The Empress, The Emperor and The Pope express the values of tradition and self-discipline to initiate us into the realms of the material, psychological and spiritual worlds. The experiences, rules, routine and order can be demanding and even claustrophobic but without our acceptance, we cannot progress.

Number V represents the four elements plus the spiritual realm of ether.

VI The Lover

The central figure is The Lover. He is youthful with a head of abundant golden hair and wears no hat (has he lost The Magician's sense of the infinite?). His multi-coloured tunic implies he is uncertain about his mode of thinking, feeling and attitude towards life but he is grasping a golden girdle (his gut feelings) with his right hand. His nakedness from the waist down accentuates a youthful vulnerability and lack of wealth. Here is a confused person: should he go with the younger woman who may promise him a temporal life of sensual bodily comforts or follow the older, wiser woman on his right whose restraining hand gently rests on his shoulder. The young woman's gestures appear to be demanding him to make a choice. His feet are pointing in opposite directions telling us he is racked with indecision as to which path to follow. He is at a crossroads: which path will he take – virtue or vice, temporal or eternal, love or fear? If he chooses fear, his path will be negative, implosive and remain in the dark. If he chooses love (meaning that aspect of Divine Love which manifests itself as 'love of

Figure 7: VI The Lover

the Self within the self', or respect for the body as the 'temple of spirit' – not to be confused with 'narcissism'), his path will be positive, expansive and in the light. The dilemma is that the price of free will is *responsibility* and the fear of knowing that every choice we make inevitably has consequences.

Above him a cherub is about to fire an arrow of love (or lust) and yet the white shaft suggests it will bring about his transformation. Is this cherub the mischievous and wilful Amor-like god who creates confusion and never grows up, or could it be The Lover's guardian angel (his higher self)? Either way, the creature is obscuring the light of the Sun (consciousness and clarity of mind). The Lover's face, although full of longing, is looking to the older woman: will she prevent him from taking any rash decision, and will he commit himself to a path of freedom through maturity and wisdom?

If the negative path of self-indulgence is followed, it will lead to disruption, frustrating inertia and fatigue in forever searching for the mythical *tall, dark stranger* who will resolve all our diffficulties.

An old Roman myth tells us about the god who became enraged by some misdemeanour of the first human mortal who, at that time, was a creature who possessed one body with two heads and two sets of arms and legs. In his rage the god took a cleaver and chopped the mortal in two. Both halves ran off in opposite directions and, ever since, each half has been searching the world to find the other half he or she belongs to.

There is no loss of 'masculinity' in a man who seeks or has found and expresses the Feminine Principle of intuition, Yin, the Moon and right-brain modes. The 'macho' man will always be 'one-sided', unless all the masculine symbols of Logos, Apollo, Yang, the Sun and left-brain modes become balanced with the feminine. The same applies equally to women, who need to bring into balance the traits of the Masculine Principle. When these two principles are integrated, the person becomes androgynous; it ends the striving to seek 'out there' his perfect woman or her perfect man, because the missing 'she' or 'he' is discovered to already exist within ourself. Once this dynamic balance has been attained, the 'perfect other half' will appear.

The number VI symbolizes a marriage and creativity. Here, The Lover has the opportunity to integrate the Masculine and Feminine Principles by drawing to himself the intuition of the anima and consummate the sacred marriage. This is the time for him to accept and value the process rather than having pre-conceived expectations and hoped-for-outcomes.

To progress on the path we need tenacity, commitment and courage.

VII The Chariot

The neophyte Lover has become a Charioteer. He is still a beardless, youthful person with flowing golden hair but has earned the right to be a young pretender to the throne and wear a coronet. In his right

Figure 8: VII The Chariot

hand he carries the semblance of an orb and sceptre (minus the cross of spirituality); his left hand holds his golden girdle and he wears the costume and breastplate of a warrior. The red-faced epaulettes on his shoulders represent the family armorial bearings intended to vigilantly guard and protect his flanks. These faces are gazing upward but the draped canopy obscures the limitless sky or upper realms. The four columns may represent the four rivers of paradise or, in this case, the four elements supporting the fifth element of ether.

The Chariot is a vehicle to take him on a journey into unfamiliar territory. He has reached the point where he has the courage to release the reins to allow the pair of horses (instinctive life force) to take him to an unknown destination. He is looking to his right and although both animals are heading in the same direction as the Charioteer, the hooves of the blue horse are veering the other way and about to explore the fertile land beneath them.

The wheel in the background indicates the cyclical rhythms of Nature – and Fate? (The significance of the emblem on the chariot has yet to be revealed but, generally, shields symbolize the protection of the ego.)

Having relinquished all resistance he embarks on a journey, conveyed by his basic instincts. Inevitably he will experience the conflict between a desire for security and control and a deep-seated need (or compulsion) to discard caution and fear by following the path that will/might lead him to his higher self-understanding and freedom. Although he is still a young, relatively immature man and knows he has a long way to go on this lonely journey, he has learned from the earlier teachings and training from the archetypes of the preceding cards and has now resolved to 'flee the nest'. If he lacks the self-confidence to travel alone, then he will not progress and all that he has been through and achieved so far will be wasted or misused for negative purposes. The neophyte must forego acting the naïve, eternal youth.

Options can dissipate the energies, but once a decision has been made it immediately concentrates the energy and focuses on the desired outcome.

The Chariot brings to an end the first of the three phases of the path of transformation – i.e. the process of learning and confronting the fear of stepping into unknown territory. This also marks the end of childhood and childishness.

VIII Justice

Justice is balanced, unbiased and fair, favouring neither left nor right but looking at us straight in the eye. The flesh-coloured hair gives the impression that she is asexual except, like The Empress, she sits poised on the throne with open thighs. The heavy crown denotes her high-ranking status but the soft, cushion-like lower part separates her head and heart from the upper crown design which is more akin to a tradi-

Figure 9: VIII Justice

tional insignia of royalty. In other words, her function is not influenced by the temporal, political affairs of state. Held upright in her right hand is the Sword of Truth and in her left hand she carries the scales that weigh the balance of law, order, compassion and forgiveness.

Her blue mantle and red cotte are similar to those worn by The High Priestess except that her kirtle undergarment is gold and it seems her feet are firmly grounded on the soil. The gold neckband and decorated collar signify her position of authority and her golden seat repeats the curved-back form of the thrones of the High Priestess and The Empress – a form of throne that appears in late-13th/early-14th-century paintings of the Madonna and Child by Cimabue and Duccio.

Justice is the balance of forces that create harmony, forthrightness and fairness, and forge an enduring link between the temporal realm of The Empress and The Emperor and the spiritual realm of The High Priestess and The Pope.

Number VIII marks the beginning of a new octave and the beginning of the second stage of the path – i.e. the steps that lead to 'clarity of mind'. Here the neophyte must learn to take responsibility for his/her every thought, deed and contractual agreement or promise – whether implied, oral or written – and to accept there will always be consequences.

Without Justice there can only be chaos, dishonour and untruths – a situation in which we become the cause of our own undoing. In other words, our lives must be governed by order and by respect for certain limitations and restraints, and for family obligations and relationships.

VIIII The Hermit

The Hermit is an old man of wisdom and knowledge. His flesh-coloured face, flowing hair and full beard are similar to the colourings of Justice and, like The Pope, suggest he has been – and still is – on a long pilgrimage. He wears no crown or headpiece to display a temporal office or status. In his left hand he holds a crooked staff to signify that the route he must take to reach his goal is not a straightforward path. In his white-sleeved right hand, partly concealed by the blue mantle, he holds a lighted lamp that will illuminate the right-handed path he must follow. The mantle also serves to conceal the ancient wisdom from the uninitiated and the profane.

The red habit and hood, typically worn by 14th-century hermits and monks, distinguish him as a man of contemplation and meditation who seeks a silent, quiet solitude to discover personal insights to throw light on his *shadow* and to discover the eternal core of his being.

If we are afraid of solitude we call it *loneliness* and become prone to dissipate energies on empty chatter, superficiality and self-deception.

Number VIIII indicates a time to pause, reflect and withdraw to appraise our inner strengths, our innate inner wisdom; to become self-reliant and to review where we now stand.

Figure 10: VIIII The Hermit

X The Wheel of Fortune

The six-spoked wheel represents the endless cycles of life and the Cosmos. No-one is turning the white handle – it is in the hands of Fate to determine and control our colour, creed, parents, status and so on. Perched on top of the wheel is a strange creature – a combination of a winged, animalistic body and a near-human, monkey-like face looking straight ahead. It is wearing a golden miniature coronet (we are ruled by Fate) and holds a white sword of transformation. Balanced on a golden shelf there appears to be a brake where the crowned animal arbitrarily acts as the controller.

On each side of the wheel are two more fabulous creatures representing the principles of good and evil (Anubis and Typhon), who manipulate the changes of fortune, but the white background suggests that anything and everything has endless possibilities.

In 1505, Machiavelli wrote, 'I think it may be the case that Fortune is the mistress of one half of our actions, and yet leaves control of the other half, or less, to ourselves.'[3] This suggests that a person's personality traits can influence how they respond to what fate has bestowed upon them. There are those who analyse, act and learn from experience, and believe there is a connection between their attitudes and what happens to them; yet there are others who believe they have no control over whatever happens to them, passively accept their fate and search for someone or something to blame instead of learning from the outcome. In other words, 'Luck' can be a triumph of Nurture over Nature. The question is: do we suffer as a victim or do we treat fatalistic disappointments, betrayals and illnesses as our teachers of important lessons to guide us further in our quest? Right

Figure 11: X The Wheel of Fortune

attitude avoids suffering. Fortune will not desert the person whose inner resolve and self-awareness are stronger than all the challenges fate has to offer.

Number X is about Karma, the Law of Compensation. Detachment from the exoteric world leads to a deepened understanding of what is going on around us and the ability to respond appropriately to events.

XI Force

The woman's serene face is looking down and to her left. Her hair, hands, lower sleeves and shoe are a natural flesh colour. The decorative, swirling, ribboned figure-of-eight hat, similar to The Magician's, symbolizes infinite potential, and the semblance of a crown suggests

Figure 12: XI Force

her high ranking status in the order of the cards. She wears a red over-mantle that is reminiscent of the copes worn by the male figures of The Emperor and The Pope, but the simple blue cotte, gold kirtle undergarment and lace-up bodice also portray the feminine attributes of The Empress. She stands firm, exuding a power of courage and strength. With her bare hands she is taming a ferocious golden lion to overcome the brute force of the beast for the same reason that Theseus had to enter the labyrinth to slay the Minotaur (*see* page 11). Mastering the inner animal instincts is a prerequisite to becoming a 'man/woman of knowledge' (*see* page 20). If we don't have the courage and endurance to overcome our fears and be prepared to uncover whatever lurks in the *shadow*, we cannot reach the goal of freedom and wisdom.

Number XI, known as the *Mandorla* is the gateway to heaven, symbolizing God (destiny) plus unity. It is the critical turning point in our journey at which we must look within to confront the *shadow*. Force is the card in the pivotal, mid-point position at the centre of a spread of 21 cards: it is a metaphor for the mid-life crisis when we ask: 'Who am I?', 'Where am I going?' and 'What is my destiny?'

XII The Hanged Man

The man is a relatively youthful, beardless person with a full, halo-like head of blue hair (intuition?). He is staring straight ahead but passively suspended upside down in time and space. His hands are held or tied behind his back; he is hanging by his left ankle, while his right leg dangles in an 'S' pattern similar to that of The Emperor, except that the latter's right leg is in front of his left. The short hooppelande tunic and hose (fashionable in the late 14th century), the white collar, the band of buttons on the blouse and the white belt suggest that the symbols of transformation run from his throat to his groin and around his solar plexus. The knotted rope is like an umbilical cord that ties him to his conditioning and previous experiences of life. His head is in a trough at ground level yet the green soil and the bar from which he is suspended are producing fertile trees. Although the trunks have sharp thorns, they are shoots of new growth.

Figure 13: XII The Hanged Man

Since passing through the stage represented by Force and experiencing all the trauma and revelation that mark the beginning of the process of self-discovery, The Hanged Man's world has been completely turned around: all that he stood for, his opinions, ideas and values are no longer valid. He is now transfixed, trapped and in danger of being wounded on the thorns. Nothing is familiar to him any longer; but, in fact, nothing has actually changed except his *point of view*! His obvious inertia gives him time to carefully contemplate and reassess his life thus far as a prelude to escaping his present paralysis and acquiring the ability to overturn his predicament. The hands concealed behind his back suggest that he has lost his sense of personal, material possessions because he is about to renounce the rule of gold in favour of the golden rule.

Number XII is about time, space and cosmic order; it is about constant change and transition. If The Hanged Man sacrifices his ego-self, reviews any outmoded behaviour and looks at life from a different viewpoint, his 'world' will change too. When the card is turned upside down he becomes a happy dancer who is about to resume his journey into the unknown and bring order out of chaos.

XIII Death

Death is an inevitable transformation from one realm to another. Skeletons lose the clothing of concealment because death cannot be dressed up!

This card does not herald a physical death. Rather, in psychological terms, it is the symbolic *death* of the ego-centred 'I' and the world of self-illusions – we need to 'die' before we can be reborn.

Figure 14: XIII Death

The skeleton moves to its left, slicing up body parts, including its own foot. It crushes the head of a young woman and decapitates a crowned male (we need to look where we are going, review what we cling on to and reassess our thought processes before we can move on). The scythe's handle reminds us of The Fool's staff and the red crescent-shaped blade may be the crystallizing power of Moon. The black soil represents both the darkness of our own *shadow* and the fear of loss of the 'I' identity.

Number XIII symbolizes God (eternity) plus resolution. Death is the passing through a closing door that ends one era or way of life to enter a new, transformed existence of regeneration that will overcome fears and inner dread.

XIIII Temperance

This angelic female character is looking down and to her right. She has the same blue-coloured hair as the older woman on The Lover's right and The Hanged Man. The red rose in her hair and the display of flesh between her breasts suggest menstrual blood and fertile creativity, sexual mysteries and the flower of a goddess. Whilst she appears to be standing firmly on the ground amongst lush green plantings, she also has wings to transport her above the material plane. Her red kirtle undergarment and sleeveless blue cotte are similar to those of the older woman in The Lover, but here Temperance is swathed in a gold, wimple-like neckpiece of *intuition* around her throat and an elaborate gold girdle of *logic* or *gut feelings* around her solar plexus. These and the red and blue chalices flowing with the white elixir of transformation symbolize the dynamic blending of life-giving alchemical substances that can be created by the blending of the Masculine and Feminine Principles. Through her feminine healing energies and heaven-sent moments of magic a new realm can be experienced.

Like number VII The Chariot, number XIIII marks the end of another octave. It is the end of old ways of thinking and behaviour and the beginning of a new octave in which we are able to exercise a clarity of mind.

Figure 15: XIIII Temperance

XV The Devil

The Devil has the smiling, cross-eyed face of a maniac who taunts the captives under his control. This androgynous figure with female breasts and male genitals has the blue wings of a monster (or is this a being from the higher worlds?). The golden headpiece of animalistic horns or some form of chaotic organic growth implies mental confusion. His hands and feet are non-human and the red girdle around his lower abdomen and the blue leggings suggest a strong sexual energy and hedonistic tendencies. He is standing on a mound of flesh-coloured substance held in a red cauldron (an emotional melting pot?). However, despite this card's apparent negativity, the white wand in his left hand repeats the symbolism of the stick held by The Fool, Amor's arrow aimed at The Lover, and the wand held by the

Figure 16: XV The Devil

creature on top of The Wheel of Fortune which suggests that The Devil holds the promise of transformation.

The naked male and female figures have animalistic ears, tails and feet; their red and black headgear with its horns or foliage signals potential growth. They are standing on black soil which, as in the pictograph of Death, promises the possibility of rebirth indicated by the fertile golden landscape in the distance. Both characters are tethered to the cauldron with flesh-coloured rope. (Is this also the cauldron of regeneration?) Like The Hanged Man, they too have their hands tied or held behind their backs, unable to grasp the opportunities offered by their innate gifts and talents. They are capable of untying the ropes that bind them but, as they now stand, they appear to be in thrall and admiration of the manipulative entity above that overpowers them.

This card marks the beginning of the most testing part of the journey. We have overcome our fears, acquired a clarity of mind and now we have power: will we be tempted to misuse it to manipulate and control others, or will our clarity of mind and power be used for higher attainment?

When we are under the influence of The Devil, it can feel as though we are carrying a depressive, ever-present burden or are being strangled by the millstones of self-doubt. This creates a personal hell in which we are in bondage to our own *shadow* and trapped by materialistic pursuits and motives. The Devil within must be confronted, otherwise our negative doubts and corruption of power will block any further progress along these final stages on the path. Regression is caused by human frailty.

Number XV represents unity plus the five elements, therefore we must aspire to a positive, inner resolve.

XVI The Tower of Destruction

Shaped like the battlements of a fortress to defend our proud ego, the over-large crown – a symbol of status, pomp, self-aggrandizement and our 'crowning achievements' – is toppled by a lightning strike from above. Whilst all the self-illusions that exist in our head are being toppled to bring us 'down-to-earth' the core of our being, the eternal core of our being – our divine essence, represented here by the main body of the tower – remains steadfast, upright and indestructible. When the ego-self is discarded the divine nature of Man stands firm.

The three windows – a pair of eyes and a larger 'third eye' – allow light to penetrate into the inner darkness, and through them we can perceive both the outer and inner worlds. The two figures crashing head-first to the ground have the blue hair, tunics, hose and footwear reminiscent of The Hanged Man, but as they fall on to undulating, rich, golden and fertile land they are being showered with raindrops from above. The pair of white stones at the base of the tower is also a portentous sign that the chaotic destruction will have a positive outcome.

Figure 17: XVI The Tower of Destruction

In the mythical story of Psyche and Amor, a Tower was Psyche's final saviour (*see* page 13). On the other hand, hubris, over-confidence, pride and a false sense of invulnerability brought about the downfall of the Tower of Babel.

Number XVI (unity plus marriage) is about achieving a Heaven on Earth. If we are to sustain a defence against all the negative aspects represented by The Devil and proceed forward, there must be a breakdown of the old order of egocentricity in order to understand our limitations and seek Truth through humility. We can then move on.

XVII The Star

This naked, voluptuous female figure embracing the essence of Nature is a combination of Mother Earth and Aphrodite. She has an abundance of the long, flowing blue hair that can be seen in The Lover, The Hanged Man, Temperance, The Tower and Judgement. The blue echoes the waters of the lake and the water pouring from the red containers. The containers also reflect the pattern of the red and blue chalices in Temperance, but here The Star is bringing the mysterious, alchemical, white elixir down to an Earthly plane.

Through her humanness, her intuition and love of Nature, she feeds the river of Life and thus both replenishes and sustains the land in the distance to produce fertile and fruitful growth. Perched on a tree, a bird of peace and heavenly flight brings a message that spirit flows through all things.

Figure 18: XVII The Star

This scene of self-nurturing and infinite care of the natural world is illuminated by a brightly shining star, surrounded by seven smaller stars to remind us that the rhythms of life are fundamental to our relationship with the Cosmos – we all come from stardust.

Number XVII is about immortality. We can no longer be solely concerned with our own life; we must become involved with our local and global environment. Our ambitions must extend beyond our self so that we will tread lightly on the planet to protect our heritage and our own human existence.

XVIII The Moon

The human face of the 'Man in the Moon' seems bemused with emotional uncertainty. The Moon's light is a reflection of the rays of the Sun, but in this card the Sun is eclipsed so we must beware of illusion, loss of clarity, deviation and being 'left in the dark'. The angelic beings in The Lover and Judgement also obscure the Sun to guard us against being overwhelmed by its rays. The howling dogs are a warning to beware of self-deception and becoming 'moonstruck'. Below them, lurking in the pool of emotion, is a lobster-like prehistoric creature with a hard outer shell to protect us from our deep-set fear of vulnerability.

The twin towers signal the need for balance in all our dealings, as already expressed by similar pairs in The Pope, Justice and The Hanged Man. Our steadfastness and core of being are also depicted in The Tower of Destruction.

The raindrops flowing upward from the Earth suggest that we should pay attention to being in touch with nature and the natural elements of our instincts and psyche. Ocean tides, menstrual flow, animal instinctiveness and human 'lunacy' are governed by the phases of the Moon.

The Moon personifies intuition, creative thought-patterns and the collective unconscious of human society, thus symbolizing the integration of the Masculine and Feminine Principles while suggesting that feminine intuition should predominate over rationality.

Number XVIII symbolizes the concept of Unity plus Heaven and

Figure 19: XVIII The Moon

Earth and the reflection of divine wisdom. The symbolism of the number XVIII is reinforced by the 19 'raindrops' – eight blue, six red and five yellow/gold. Nineteen has always been considered by the sages to be a mystical number, being the number of years it takes for the Moon to orbit around the Sun and return to its original position.

XVIIII The Sun

In all its glory, The Sun smiles, showering the World with light and nature's blessings and vitality. Life's energies 'rain' down from the Heavens above along alternating straight and curved rays that reflect the principal colours of the other cards: gold, blue, red, green and white.

Two naked innocents (Anima and Animus; heart and mind),

Figure 20: XVIIII The Sun

wearing blue loincloths for modesty, are tenderly touching each other in close affection, their feet firmly on the ground. They may represent the child within us emerging out of the shadow and into the light, exposing our inner self with nothing to hide. Behind is a golden brick wall with a red coping to protect the children. (The myth of Prometheus, who was burned when he flew too close to the Sun, tells us that worldly success is but short-lived.) The 13 raindrops remind us that the 13th card, Death, is also an illusion that is negated by the eternal power and blessing of the Sun which transforms and illuminates the Moon – the unconscious self.

Number XVIIII is a mystical, enigmatic number that figures in many spiritual texts and signals the emergence of *self* from the *shadow* to *become that which we already are.*

XX Judgement

Like the winged angelic figure in The Lover, here is another partly human, partly divine creature with a saintly halo above its head, obscuring the full orb of the Sun. It has flesh-coloured wings, rather than the blue of the cherub's wings, and bursts out of blue clouds.

The 'Angel' is sounding a horn to celebrate success and the triumphant awakening and rebirth of the person rising from the ground. The gold cross on a white banner represents the cross of redemption and destiny. The banner can also represent the active/passive principles and the 'World Axis' as a bridge for the soul to discover its Self. The golden hair is a reminder of the earlier incarnations of The Magician, The Chariot and The Lover.

The Sun is obscured by the blue cloud from out of which the

Figure 21: XX JUDGEMENT

'Angel' emerges, reminding us that the power and light of the Sun (ego) can consume itself unless it is moderated by the angelic heavenly realms of our higher Self. The three earthly figures form a trinity of mind, body and spirit – an awakening and liberation from terrestrial limitations.

Below the 'Angel' are naked figures: one is female with the blue hair of Temperance and The Star and the other, an older, wiser man has the long blue hair of The Hanged Man. They are in prayerful pose of thanksgiving and blessings, facing a third person emerging from the depths of the green, fertile soil. This androgynous figure wears a blue hat that is similar to those worn by The Pope's disciples.

These naked figures personify The Fool, The Magician and The Lover. They emerge from a rectangular tomb to become reborn as mature, evolved, fully-realized beings.

The imagery on this card, similar to The Resurrection of the Dead seen on the south porch at Chartres Cathedral in France, can also be found in many other medieval paintings and sculptured reliefs of the Last Judgement. This is the Day of Judgement when we come to terms with having learned the Truth about who we are without fear or remorse. Part of our quest is to live by grace.

Number XX concerns separation plus zero or eternity and the mysteries of the unknown: we are separated from the unknowable.

XXI The World

The naked, now fully expressed female, is completely open and transparent to the world. She dances on her right leg with the left leg tucked behind, forming the figure 'S' (the divine fire of the heart) but in an opposite stance to those of The Emperor and The Hanged Man. Like The Magician, she holds a wand in her left hand. The flesh-coloured ribbons remind us of the drapery on the thrones of The High Priestess and The Empress and the hats worn by The Magician and Force, which are shaped to form a lemniscate, the symbol of eternity. She is inside the *Vesica Piscis*-shaped laurel wreath of success and victory which is also known as the 'gateway to Heaven'. The wreath

Figure 22: XXI The World

forms a boundary or limitation on matter and represents the journey coming 'full circle', uniting the colours red, blue and gold.

On the four corners are the bull, the lion, the eagle and an angelic being representing the four elements of earth, fire, water and air and our modes of sensing, intuiting, thinking and feeling – all symbolizing the dancer's integration of the four aspects of Cosmic order. She personifies the archetypal world through her self-discipline and self-knowledge by acting out her personal myth to achieve joy and fulfilment – 'The days of thy mourning shall be ended'. The figures on the four corners often appear in the sculpture and decoration of medieval cathedrals, and can be seen on the West Front at Chartres where they are placed in the identical positions to this card around the figure of Christ in a mandorla. In the Christian tradition they are said to represent the four evangelists: bull = Luke; lion = Mark; eagle = John; man/angel = Matthew.

Number XXI is separation plus unity, therefore the outer world (our 'personal world') is reunited with our inner world and we have become aware of and understood the realities of time, the spiritual and material realms, and Cosmic laws.

The World is but a short-lived culmination of our quest because the upward spiral of the journey begins all over again to take us to another, yet higher level.

DECODING THE MINOR ARCANA

THE NUMBERED CARDS

The 56 Minor Arcana cards are thought to represent the sum total of life's experiences. This number has other correspondences: the ancient astronomical Great Year consisted of 56 years, and the Solar and Lunar cycles coincide every 56 years. Fifty-six was the Natal number of the Sun God born to Mother Earth (Tara). Buddha's first 56 steps were 14 (seven forward, seven backward) in each direction to form a cross, and there were 56 postholes forming the Aubrey Circle at Stonehenge to mark the solar and lunar eclipses. There are, of course, other systems proposed by various authorities and these will be found in books such as Manly P Hall's *The Secret Teachings of All Ages* (see Bibliography).

Readers who use the Tarot for prediction and fortune telling see the numbered suit cards as actual events that may happen in the future. For example, the Six of Cups foretells a pending marriage or a new baby; the One or Ace of Money means an unexpected gift is on its way, and so on. The alternative, non-predictive 'reading' views the numbered suit cards as events in our daily lives that can influence the way we react to given situations. These cards thus present us with insightful opportunities to become aware of our usual mode of thinking and responding to given situations. If we are receptive and non-judgemental, such insights can help to bring about beneficial changes along the path to self-awareness. To illustrate this we can take the example of a child being sent away to school. The emotional impact of such an event may cause one child to feel abandoned and unloved, whereas another child's response may be one of pleasure and relief to be out of the control of the parents. Yet another child may appreciate the sacrifice the parents have made to enable him or her to go to a better school or improved environment. The actual *event* is simply that the child has gone away to school, but how that event is interpreted can either cause emotional trauma and stress or it can be treated as an exciting adventure. In other words, it is not the event but our often automatic response to it that can cause a range of emotions ranging from sorrow or self-pity to pleasure.

Below is a suggested synthesis of the conventional number symbolism, including the Hermetic Laws listed on page 35, that may be applied to the Tarot's Minor Arcana card numbers. Each card has both a positive and a negative connotation which may be helpful in the context of the card expressing a value in relationship to other cards in terms of syntax and semantics when reading a spread.

Number One

KEY WORDS: The Source; Divine Spirit; Oneness; Natural Gifts

Number one represents the unity and oneness of the Cosmos – expressed as 'God' or the eternal spirit that is present in all things, the seed from which everything stems – order, originality, creativity and endless possibilities. This number encapsulates all our natural talents and blessings held in potential. In other words, the Universe – God if you will – has offered us gifts and abilities to enable us, as CG Jung put it, 'to become that which we already are'.

Number one is a principle rather than a number that marks the beginning and permeates all things. It expresses something absolute, expansiveness, and the undivided self in a state of bliss.

ANTITHESIS: We may not be using or exploring our gifts and talents and are perhaps misusing them for negative purposes.

There may be confusion about which path to follow, or we may even be living in a fool's paradise. Instead of expanding we are imploding, contracting or hiding ourselves.

Number Two

KEY WORDS: Duality; Separation; Creativity

Number two expresses the Feminine Principle of intuition, the womb of life, creativity and a desire for peace and harmony, but it also symbolizes duality and polarity expressed as Yin and Yang, light and dark, night and day, life and death, active and passive. The Hermetic *Law of Polarity* is about opposites; being in conflict; sitting on different sides of the table in a state of argument.

Separation from our true spirit or nature leads to a realization that we are not 'complete' or fulfilled. So, where do we focus our energies, and how or where can we find the inner lover?

ANTITHESIS: There is a need to be decisive to search for ways to heal a rift; to find a way to re-integrate with oneself and to recognize that the contrasts may be too accentuated. There may be too much light or too much darkness.

Number Three

KEY WORDS: Reconciliation; Soul Fulfilment

Number three expresses the Masculine Principle of rationality, prudence and a sense of completion. It also expresses the masculine life-force and sexual libido. Three is about the integration of mind, body and spirit and the joy of using positive energies and sexual power.

The *Law of Resonance* is about harmony, resolution and reconciliation, where two people stand side by side – not on opposite sides – using debate to find a truth (the third component) rather than trying to argue that black is white. Number three is a symbol of going forth and living in a forthright manner.

ANTITHESIS: Impotence, ignorance, malice and an inability to complete or resolve outstanding issues. It may represent inertia and withdrawal.

Number Four

KEY WORDS: Materiality; Earthiness; Endurance

Number four is symbolic of the four elements – fire, air, water and earth – that constitute the material world and Cosmic order. The four elements can also represent intuition (fire), thinking (air), feeling (water) and sensation (earth) and symbolize the inspirational, cultural, social and physical planes of existence.

The four segments to the Hermetic *Law of Manifestation* refer to the four elements:

First there is the element of Fire which is that spark of *genius*, that brilliant imaginative idea or creative thought that has come from nowhere – *out of the blue.*

Then follows the element of Air which is symbolic of the *thinking* process. Who are the people such as professional advisers, craftsmen, specialists, or what are the tools or finances needed to bring forth the idea?

The next element, Water, is about *formation*: to create a two-dimensional plan or model of what form this idea will take because any manifestation must have three dimensions. At this stage we need to imagine it in our mind's eye or sketch it on paper or simulate it using computer graphics.

The final process is the Earth element. This is where the *idea* is about to be manifested or actually built in three dimensions. We may all have bright ideas and creative imaginings but how many become a manifested reality? The difficulty is that as we go through each element so the resistance increases and this can only be overcome by our commitment, tenacity and will power.

ANTITHESIS: There may be a tendency to hold on too tenaciously to our worldly goods, or there may be a negative energy preventing us from getting our life in order. We must beware of being too earthbound and never dream of other realms or lose our sense of the reality of the inner worlds.

Number Five

KEY WORDS: Humankind; Hope and Humanity; Uncertainty

The fifth element added to fire, air, water and earth is the quintessential element of ether or the *heavenly realm*. Human beings are composed of a gross (material) body made up of the four elements plus the subtle body of ether (spirit).

Number five (two representing female + three representing male) is the sigil of Man, humankind, human nature and natural phenomena. It symbolizes the full spectrum of life and living, of sensual pleasures and enjoyment, because spirit has tempered the four elements of materiality.

Number five can signify hope and endeavour.

ANTITHESIS: Paucity of life; disregard of nature and the environment. It may indicate a certain recklessness or lack of a sense of humanity.

Number Six

KEY WORDS: Harmony; Balance; Stability

Number six is made up of two (female) + three (male) + one (unity or a child). It is a symbol of harmony, marriage, love, beauty and resolution. It represents partnership, health and a balance of mind, body and spirit. As with all partnerships, marriages or the birth of a child, we are vulnerable, embarking on an adventure to an unknown destination, but we must be prepared to trust in the outcome.

ANTITHESIS: We may feel we are at a crossroads and cannot decide which route to take. Unforeseen, unexpected circumstances could upset the equilibrium of our life which could create a sense of conflict.

Number Seven

KEY WORDS: Cyclical Changes; Rhythm of Life

Number seven is about the cycles of time, cosmic order, the changing rhythms of the seasons and possible changes in fortune and to transformation.

There are the seven days of the week, the seven colours of the rainbow, the seven musical notes, the seven Liberal Arts (grammar, rhetoric, logic, arithmetic, geometry, music and cosmology) and so on.

ANTITHESIS: Disorder, chaos, bareness, a lack of or disjointed movement. There may be too much or not enough time and an absence of control or discipline. The natural flow and rhythm of life may be temporally disrupted.

Number Eight

KEY WORDS: Judgement; Regeneration; Material and Spiritual Success

Number eight can represent law, justice, prudence and a balance of seemingly opposing forces.

The octave can signal the start of something new: perhaps regeneration or a renewed endeavour combining the energies of Heaven and Earth. It represents the culmination of worldly goods and spirit or inner fulfilment.

Number eight symbolizes Hermes Trismegistus' tenet 'as above, so below'. It is also the goal of the initiate.

ANTITHESIS: A sense of incompleteness; stagnation; unfairness and dissatisfaction.

Number Nine

KEY WORDS: Human Frailty; Detachment; Review of Attainments

Number nine is the bridge to another realm: it signifies being on the brink of something new. But we need to exercise caution or mark a pause, allowing time for consolidation or reflection and the gaining of insights into our positive experiences and shortcomings. This is a period to allow space and time for new ideas to emerge; a time for preparation that has the potential for new discoveries and self-understanding.

ANTITHESIS: A sense of a lack of progress, inertia and dissatisfaction due to unexplored talents and abilities. There may be limitations and difficulty in seeing a way forward.

Number Ten

KEY WORDS: Transition; Purpose; Fulfilment

Number ten – the Decad – embraces all numbers and is complete at four $(1 + 2 + 3 + 4 = 10)$: unity (one), duality (two), reconciliation (three) and the manifest world (four) represent cosmic creativity.

Nature is God (one) + infinity (zero) = spiritual law. Number ten is a turning point when all things are possible. This may be a time to begin again with a greater sense of trust and effort but without becoming overburdened.

ANTITHESIS: This signals a period when we need to get back to basics and to understand our limitations. We must take care of the necessities of life – including our spiritual needs.

THE FOUR SUITS

The interpretation and meaning of each numbered card in the Minor Arcana are moderated by the symbolic quality of each of the four suits – Money, Cups, Swords and Clubs – which correspond respectively to materiality, emotions (or feelings), intellect and creativity / energy. These four suits are related to the four suits of ordinary playing cards – Diamonds, Hearts, Spades and Clubs – which are believed to have been invented for overtly innocent games to avoid religious prosecution whilst still maintaining the encoded teachings from the time when Tarot cards were banned.

The four suits of the Minor Arcana cards are called:

Money	(also called Coins or Pentacles)
Cups	(also called Chalices)
Swords	
Clubs	(also called Wands, Batons or Rods)

These suits correspond to the four elements Earth, Water, Air and Fire which in turn relate to materiality, emotions, the mind and spirit. In medicine they are known as the four Humours – Melancholic, Phlegmatic, Sanguine and Choleric.

For the key words, *see* chapter 3, The Language of the Tarot (pages 29–46).

The Suit of Money *The Earth element*

KEY: Sensing and mastery of the physical body

This suit reflects our material, manifested world, our relative comforts, earthiness, sensuousness and the desire for security, money and worldly possessions. It concerns the five senses and the quintessence of life – the four elements plus ether. Here we are dealing with structure, stability, the practicalities of life and living and being 'down to earth', and how we perceive the physical world of the senses.

ANTITHESIS: The negative aspects can be over-indulgence, greed, dullness, stubbornness and one-track materialism.

The Suit of Cups: *The Water element*

KEY: The realm of emotions and the full range and depth of our feelings

The Cup or Grail is a divine vessel, symbolic of the primordial cosmic womb and the search for the secret of immortal life. The suit of Cups relates to our love of nature and our nurturing attitudes while reflecting our close relationships and feelings – from the calm waters of a lake to the raging storms of the sea. Water is the source of all existence on Earth and the flow of the river of life that carries us on our journey. It has cleansing properties. Water also takes the form of that which contains it, indicating that it represents formation and shape.

ANTITHESIS: The negative aspects are over-sensitivity, manipulative moodiness, self-pity and a tendency to be constantly overwhelmed with emotional stress.

The Suit of Swords: *The Air element*

KEY: Rationality and intellectual powers

This suit represents the Masculine Principle, incisiveness, mental agility, clarity of mind and reasoning. A sword symbolizes powers of thinking and logic and it can cut and thrust to get through the 'red tape'; but if used indiscriminately in adversarial confrontation, its double-edge can cause unnecessary wounding and be unjust.

ANTITHESIS: The negative aspects are lack of feeling and compassion, subversive aggression, verbal attack and viciousness. (It is better to give someone a piece of your heart than a piece of your mind.)

The Suit of Clubs: *The Fire element*

KEY: Inspiration, creativity and intuition

This suit represents the Feminine Principle and reflects our energy, vitality, our entrepreneurial ideas, our enthusiasms, our creative imagination and optimism. Clubs can be instruments for creating magic, the spirit of life, and the passions and dreams that give birth to whatever we manifest in our life.

ANTITHESIS: The negative aspects are boredom, disruptive hyperactivity, inability to focus, lack of mental discipline and a tendency to use energies and talents for negative purposes and domination. A club can be used as a blunt instrument.

THE NUMBER/SUIT MATRIX

Most if not all designers of modern packs introduce pictographs for each of the numbered cards. These illustrations impose the designer's own very specific ideas which allow only one possible interpretation or meaning for each of the numbered cards. As with the older and, I believe, more authentic decks such as the *Ancien Tarot de Marseille* there are no such evocative pictographs but only the symbols of each suit which allows Tarot readers to exercise intuition to create their own unfettered interpretations. All one needs to do is study, meditate on and remember the 'qualities' of each of the numbers one to ten as set out in on pages 32–35 and then 'modify' or adjust the meanings by reference to the symbolic 'value' of the suit number as noted above.

Below is a matrix of numbers and suits to demonstrate how one can build up a personal vocabulary for each card. Again, it must be emphasized that these are not *definitive* statements, merely interpretive guides.

The keywords in the matrix are a distillation of the esoteric number symbolism set out in chapter 3, The Language of the Tarot, and in the above section 'The Four Suits'. For examples of the numbered cards – one from each suit – *see* plates 24–7.

THE COURT CARDS

There are four 'Court' cards: the Knave, the Knight, the Queen and the King (*see* plates 28–43). These cards are named but unnumbered. Generally, teachers of the Tarot suggest that the Court cards represent real personalities who are already in our lives or people we are about to meet. Bearing in mind our own unique myth set out in the Three-Act Drama of Life in chapter 2, everyone who comes into our orbit is introduced by ourselves. We may therefore look upon the 16 Court cards as being 'outer world' mirror images of the sub-personalities that inhabit our private 'inner world'. We also saw in the Three-Act Drama that sometimes the 'good guys' turn out to be 'bad guys' (and vice-versa) in varying degrees of plusses and minuses. In other words, we need to be aware of the counter-balancing 'flip-side' or negative aspects of our own and other people's characteristics.

Whether we call it fate, good luck or synchronicity, the psyche (our inner guide) attracts certain people – mother, father, sister, brother, partners, friends, enemies – into our lives for the specific purpose of reflecting ourselves to ourselves. In other words, they act as a mirror to reflect certain aspects which, if accepted and under-stood, will help us to take a step closer to self-understanding. All these characters can become invaluable teachers. Synchronicity and the Universe are ever-ready to help those who are willing to take their next step along the path. The events that befall us and all the people we will meet and have met so far should be treated as wel-come encounters.

The four suits or elements – Earth, Water, Air, Fire – are metaphors to refer to the four 'Worlds': our material world; our world of emotion and feelings; the intellectual world of our mind and our world of spirit and life-force energies. In each of these worlds or planes of existence we have latent talents and dreams (the Knave) and aspirations and ambitions (the Knight). When a Knave appears in a spread it may trigger hitherto unacknowledged gifts or abilities. Similarly, a Knight will remind us that, for a variety of 'reasons', we may aspire to do or be something that lurks in the 'back of our mind', unaware that if such

Table 1: The Number/Suit Matrix

NUMBER & KEYWORDS

	Keywords:	MONEY Sensing
Number One	The source, unity Natural gifts Ace A fortuitous event	Good fortune Talent for the good life Improvement in circumstances
Number Two	Feminine Principle Separation Duality	Difficulty in 'making ends meet' Material demands/needs not matching expectations
Number Three	Masculine Principle Reconciliation Resolution	Pleasure and satisfaction with one's material lot
Number Four	Manifestation The four elements Endurance	Tendency to be too 'down-to- earth' Attitudes becoming too materialistic
Number Five	Human nature Spirit of life force Uncertainty	Avoid over-indulgences Enjoyment of what life has to offer
Number Six	Masculine plus feminine plus child = creativity Decision time	Beneficence of Nature and the natural world Fertility
Number Seven	Rhythm of Life Cyclical changes	Changes of circumstances
Number Eight	As above, so below (Compensations, Regeneration)	New opportunities to rethink material circumstances and spiritual fulfilment
Number Nine	Detachment Consolidation Time for preparation	Pause to reassess one's personal circumstances and focus energies
Number Ten	Transition Integration Law and order	Tread lightly on the Planet

| CUPS | SWORDS | CLUBS |
Feeling	Thinking	Intuition
Inner happiness Emotional contentment	Peace of mind Clarity of mind	Inspiration Creative ideas Emergence of natural talents
Inner conflict Feeling of uncertainty	Dilemma State of indecision Illusion Caught in two minds	Creative energies need to be focused and directed
Prudence resolves emotional stress Happy outcome	Resolution of a conflict	Intuition and rationality create balance in terms of mind, body and spirit
Need/desire to make dreams a reality	Bring order, structure and practicalities into thought processes	Allow ideas and creativity to become grounded
Compassion Senses human frailties	Be tolerant of feelings and human spirit	Altruism Use energies for benefit of humankind
Family, children and close relationships	Trust in new thought patterns	Successful outcome of creative processes
Restlessness Need for emotional stimulation	Search for meaning Engage in life's rhythms and changes	Allow for cycles of energy levels
Renewed optimism Re-birth	Respect for law, order and traditional values	Introduce a wider range of energies to encompass materiality and spirit
Self-assessment Count one's blessings Acceptance	Time to reflect on thinking processes and attitudes	Recuperation to allow birth of something new
Allow time to heal past traumas and to revitalize relationships	Become aware of unexplored potentialities and purpose	Trust intuition to direct and optimize creative energies

aspirations were to manifest in our lives it would lead us closer to fulfilment. The attributes of the Queen (intuition) and the King (rationality) hold the keys.

As we shall see, the *quality* of a Court card is determined by the characteristic symbolism of each suit. Thus the Knave of Money brings to our notice an innovative idea for improving our financial status or a need to seek new horizons. The Knight of Cups might suggest that we are engrossed in our feelings or that we are, or need to be, concerned about ecology and the planet. The Queen of Swords might tell us that on certain occasions our love and compassion might be tempered better with gentle ruthlessness. The King of Clubs balances intuition with rationality, turning idealism into workable reality. Further modifications to the meaning will also be determined by the positive or negative aspects of the immediately surrounding cards in a spread.

The Court cards can tell us how our negative attitudes and game-playing are blocking our progress. We must remember that the Knight is still relatively young (naive), inexperienced and may display impetuosity. It should be noted that the four Kings, the Knight of Clubs and the Knaves of Money and Swords all wear the lemniscate style hat of The Magician and Force to warn us that whilst these 'characters' are capable of creating magic and have some understanding of the power within themselves they can also become the trickster and ruthless manipulator, cheat and liar. With the exception of the Knight of Swords, the Queen of Money and the Knave of Clubs, all the other Court card characters have white (transforming) heads of hair.

The grammar and interpretation of symbolism in the pictographs of these Court Cards – The Knave, Knight, Queen and King – are consistent with the Major cards. These 56 Minor Court and numbered cards are 'modified' by the metaphoric expression of each of the four suits, also known as the Four Paths of Illumination.

The Knave

The Knave (sometimes known as The Page) is a young person who serves a knight as a servant/message bearer and apprentice to be trained for his own eventual knighthood. He was a Jack-the-Lad character who needed to be clever and smart – even crafty and challenging in his own way. He is the personification of *potentiality* for ideas; the embryonic preparation for something new and the seeker of new horizons. The Knave prepares the ground and seeks new horizons. Of course, he is still in a relatively naïve state and might make mistakes or deliver a wrong or incomplete message because he may be confused. On the other hand, the message could be the sort of wake-up call that comes 'from the mouths of babes' or that is 'young at heart'.

ANTITHESIS: In a negative mode, he will be cunning, deceitful and remain the eternal, childish youth who never grows up and succumbs to addictions of drugs, sex or crime.

The Knight

The Knight is a spirited young pretender to the throne with tendencies to romanticism and aspirations to be a champion crusader. He seeks challenges to exercise his developing, or developed, talents and capabilities; he is a warrior, a follower of ideals and enjoys the status of being a hero who carries out good deeds and gets things done. His horse expresses his spirit of adventure. The rider (spirit) must master the horse (bodily vehicle). The Knight symbolizes thoughts and points of view rather than an actual person.

ANTITHESIS: In his negative mode the Knight may be misguided and unnecessarily expend energy on lost causes, or he may not fully appreciate or express the truth of a matter. He might be lazy, lack courage, have a tendency to dream his life away or become a bully and brutal.

The Queen

The Queen expresses the Feminine Principle of all aspects of womanhood, intuition and the nurturing of family, friends and, of course, she holds the key to the sacred marriage with the king of their realm.

ANTITHESIS: In her negative mode she can become the wicked witch, the harridan, and use her occult powers for evil purposes, indulge in emotional blackmail and either be precocious or lapse into helplessness. In this mode she is a destroyer rather than a creator. Either way, her strategies ensure she is in control of people and all situations.

The King

The King is the supreme ruler, one who knows and protects the boundaries; one who is disciplined, who governs wisely and blesses those in his realm. He expresses the mature Masculine Principle of rationality, feelings of security and justice.

ANTITHESIS: In his negative mode he can become a tyrant, a weakling, an ineffective leader with no sense of justice or discipline. He protects neither his own boundaries nor those around him.

THE SUIT OF MONEY (PLATES 28–31)

Knave of Money

The Knave is a beardless youth with his feet planted firmly on the flesh-coloured, fertile soil. His static stance is similar to The Magician's posture. He gazes intently to his right at the gold and black symbol of a coin delicately balanced on his right hand while his left hand grasps the decorated gold girdle, suggesting he has an innate 'gut feeling' for money and the material pleasures of life. The overlarge hat repeats the same symbol as The Magician, Force and the King of Money, Knight of Clubs and Knave of Swords.

The red tunic, gold girdle, blue hose and red shoes incorporate the same clothing as The Fool. Another coin disc is floating just above the ground over his right foot. ('He has the world at his feet.')

The Knave can have a tendency to become a trickster and indulge in unscrupulous dealings.

This card symbolizes a budding entrepreneurship; a latent ability to create the magic to improve material existence and enjoy the sensualities of life and living, but it remains *in potential*. In other words, the groundwork is being prepared for something new.

Knight of Money

The Knight's eyes are completely focused on the coin as both he and his horse move ahead in the same direction. He has turned in the opposite direction to the Knave and now the coin ahead has become much larger and more prominent. The Magician's hat worn by the Knave has been discarded for a more simple, practical, everyday fillet headwear, but in his right hand he holds a weighty, powerful wand as his weapon to create the magic to achieve his desires. The gold-edged red tunic, blue hose and red shoe are reminders that The Fool's influence is still present. He is mounted on a flesh-coloured horse (his spirit) with blue hooves, gold bridle and decorated girth, and both rider and steed single-mindedly go forth together.

The Knave's potentiality has become the conscious aspirations of the Knight. He knows what he wants to do and has the ability to put his thoughts into action by using the club (intuition) for practical application. His expedient thinking processes may lead him to use people and situations for his own ends: he needs to be aware that his club could become a bludgeoning weapon.

Queen of Money

The Queen stares intensely at the even bigger coin disc balanced on her over-large right hand while her normal-sized left hand lightly holds a black and gold mace. The decorated crown is precariously perched on her head and she does not appear to be sitting on her gold and green throne. She wears a flesh-coloured girdle around her waist and a matching neckpiece.

The blue hair suggests that she possesses certain characteristics of the older woman in The Lover, The Hanged Man, Temperance, The Star, The Moon and Judgement and the blue mane of the mounts of the Knights of Cups and Clubs.

This Queen has all the attributes of womanhood symbolized in the Major Arcana cards. Apart from her highly developed intuition, she personifies love, motherhood, sensuality and all the sensuousness of clothes, jewellery and a created beautiful environment. She makes the perfect mother/wife/mistress. Although she carries a mace and has a throne, the loosely worn crown indicates she is less concerned about her royal status than her ambitions to acquire security and the material blessings life has to offer.

Her ruthless drive for money and security could turn her into a greedy woman who lusts for power.

King of Money

This bearded, white-haired King is a wise old man who sits comfortably and at ease on his well-decorated and embellished throne that is more like a well-upholstered chair. He has no need to focus his energies on the smaller-sized coin he holds in his right hand and casually looks away, ignoring the money symbol. Like the Queen and the Knight, he appears to have no need for the trappings of a royal personage. Instead, he wears the hat (and attitudes) of the youthful Knave. This King knows how to create the magic of the Magician and has the experiences demanded by Force.

He is balanced on his left leg with his right crossed over in front, like The Emperor and The Hanged Man (except the latter's right leg is crossed over behind), and wears the same blue hose and red shoes of The Hanged Man. His legs form the shape of the chemical sign 'S' for Sulphur. His head is turned towards his left, looking away from the direction of his body and feet which might indicate a wise man's ability to be flexible and amenable to changing his mind.

The two legs of his throne and the flamboyant clothing suggest that his material wealth and status are only temporarily on Earth. This personification of rationality and the Masculine Principle indicates that he is a 'man of the world' whose throne is set in a natural environment. As he is looking away from the sigil of money, he may be inclined to be philanthropic because he can afford to be generous. Whilst he knows how to turn a deal to his advantage, he could become a grasping tyrant whose only interest and purpose in life is to acquire more and more material wealth.

The Knave and Queen are facing right and the Knight and King to their left suggesting that to be an entrepreneurial character in the material world one needs to exercise a subtle combination of intuition and rationality.

THE SUIT OF CUPS (PLATES 32-5)

Knave of Cups

The long, white, garlanded hair and his forlorn gaze down into the Cup suggest that his head is full of romantic, idealistic thoughts. He carries a hat in his left hand; the windswept drapery and scarf is like the gold wimple worn by Temperance and the swirling ribbon of the Queen of Cups' throne. In his right hand he carries a burdensome, heavy, over-sized Cup.

His red tunic, blue hose and red shoes express similar characteris-tics to the Knave of Money. But this Knave, ponderously trying to grasp the significance of the Cup, is certainly on the move across a gold and fertile landscape. He appears to be overwhelmed by feelings, sensitiv-ities, idealism and unrealized, probably incoherent dreams.

Knight of Cups

Like the Knave, he is still intensely focused on the Cup, totally engrossed in his feelings, except he has a longer perspective on what it might mean. The Cup itself is over-large and heavy and barely 'balanced' rather than grasped in his right hand. His mode of dress, lack of headwear and his movement to the right suggest that nothing very much has developed from being a Knave except that he is mounted on a blue-maned horse (*see above*, Queen of Money). Of all four Knights, it is only the Knight of Cups who is holding the reins of the horse: does this indicate he is controlling where his 'spirit' will take him in his quest? This may be a quest for romantic love which could evolve into him becoming a cru-sader for ecology out of a love of humanity and the Planet.

Unless he introduces order and rationality into his life the poten-tiality for manifesting his heartfelt desires will be thwarted and, out of frustration, he could turn to subversive activities.

Queen of Cups

The crown sits on a rolled, stuffed base, which separates both her head and her heart from the status and authority symbolized by the crown. This is similar to the base of the crown worn by Justice. She sits comfortably, with parted thighs, on a throne hidden from view; the flowing, ribbon-like gold and flesh-coloured drapery is reminiscent of the thrones of The High Priestess, The Empress, The World and the scarf worn by the Knave. Her red mantle, blue cotte, gold girdle and gold kirtle are also similar to those worn by The Empress, Force, Temperance and the Queen of Money. In her right hand she has a firm grasp on the Cup which has a closed lid concealing the secrets of the full spectrum of love: romantic, sexual, compassionate, unconditional love and the love of humanity. The transformational white wand she carries in her left hand can also be seen in The Fool, The Lover, The Wheel Of Fortune, The Devil and the Knight of Swords and King of Clubs. Again, as with Justice, she balances her feelings with compassion and has the power of her wand to transform our life to experience peace and love.

In her negative mode she can be floating or drowned in a sea of turmoil and uncontrolled, self-induced deep emotional stress.

King of Cups

This card is dominated by the over-sized Cup and the King's flamboyant headwear. His crown appears to have a pair of wings: does this indicate he is ungrounded with his head in the clouds? The heavy crown reminds us of The Tower of Destruction and inflated egos. He sits easily on his throne, has a firm hold on the weighty, ornate Cup and his left elbow is nonchalantly resting on the well-padded, golden arm of the throne. Like the other three Kings, he is looking to his left, disregarding the object in his right hand and turning away from the direction of his body. Unlike the Cups in the other Court cards in this suit, the Cup the king holds has no red ball decoration on its stem. His blue tunic, gold girdle and red cloak are similar to The Emperor's dress and not dissimilar to the tunic, red hose and blue shoes worn by the King of Money.

This King is capable of ruthless compassion and his strong feelings need to be tempered by rational thought. He is a caring ruler but has a tendency to lack balanced judgement to the point where he could become a weak-willed tyrant who gives in to whims, indulgences and seduction.

THE SUIT OF SWORDS (PLATES 36–9)

Knave of Swords

The knave is staring at the ground and leaning to the left in an unstable stance. Although he wears the lemniscate hat of The Magician, Force, the King and Knave of Money, and carries a sword and red staff or wand (The Fool), he appears to be unaware of the potential and potency of the gifts and talents bestowed upon him. The gold sword with a white hilt is held in such a manner that it could not be used as a weapon (for intellectual fencing); instead, he is in danger of wounding himself on the left side of his face. The sloping sword also indicates the lack of balance and discernment seen in the sword of Justice and the King of Swords. His actions, gifts and judgement could be unpredictable and he would find difficulty in directing his innate cleverness. His stance, hose and shoes are similar to the Knave of Money and the well-cut tunic (The Hanged Man) and flowing blue and gold mantle (The Hermit) suggest he may be inclined to be thoughtful about his position and enjoy solitude.

Knight of Swords

This is a young man dressed for battle, ready for action and on the move. A heavily reinforced helmet protects the most treasured part of his body. His armour, gold girdle and flesh-coloured epaulette remind us of The Emperor and The Chariot. The gold breast plate and shin guards also protect his heart and lower limbs. He is intent on upholding the law, order and traditional values. In his left hand he carries a white, transformatory sword that has the power to right the world's wrongs but it is dangerously close to the horse's head – he might wound his own spirit.

The prancing, heavily armoured horse and richly decorated girth, red saddle and regalia indicate that, like the Knave, this Knight and his horse are fashionably well dressed.

The Knight is a person with a mission who seeks both physical and intellectual challenges to satisfy his crusader spirit. Such zealous endeavours could become belligerent and unnecessarily aggressive to the point where an argument is generated simply to satisfy a need to exercise or sharpen his wits.

Queen of Swords

As with the Knave and Knight, the Queen of Swords is looking to her right. She carries a red-bladed sword which is not held upright (*see* the sword of Justice), suggesting that she may be swayed by her intuitive feelings of compassion. The crown is comparatively lightweight; her red cotte, blue, gold and flesh-coloured mantle, gold kirtle, gold neckband and girdle illustrate an attire similar to The High Priestess, Justice and Temperance.

Her gold and flesh-coloured throne, on which she sits comfortably and with her thighs apart, is similar to the throne of Justice. The left hand is touching her solar plexus indicating that she trusts her 'gut feelings'.

This is a well-organized, tidy woman whose sharp, energetic intellect is tempered by intuition. She will help to defend the realm but may find herself embroiled in lost causes and swayed by her head rather than her heart.

King of Swords

The King, a beardless, clever man who is young at heart, is half-sitting, half-standing and ready for action. Ignoring the weapon in his right hand, he is looking down to his left with his body and feet turned to the right. His elaborate lemniscate Magician's hat, far more prominent than his royal status crown, indicates that he has a bright agile mind and encourages innovative thought and ideas. The sword, with its flesh-coloured blade and gold hilt, is carried upright in his right hand and his left hand lightly holds a white and gold mace or wand. The dangerous cutting edge of the sword is prevented from causing a self-inflicted wound by the brim of his hat.

The epaulettes and armour (The Chariot and the Knight of Swords) suggest he upholds family values, tradition and the rule of law. The epaulette's face on his right shoulder has both eye and mouth closed but the face on his left shoulder has an eye and mouth open. (Does this mean he knows when to be silent and when to speak?) The well-decorated blue breastplate and gold neckpiece protect his feelings and power of speech (persuasion) and the armoured red skirt guards his sexual region. The white girdle might suggest he exercises an intuitive flexibility. His throne appears to be a hard stone plinth, decorated with an unidentified insignia: seemingly, this King is not too concerned with material comforts!

The King of Swords is a well-armed, well-prepared monarch who will fight for a just and rational cause. He has a tenacious spirit, enjoys challenges and responds positively to new ways of thinking and reasoning to achieve a goal.

In his negative mode he could be a rigid, intolerant tyrant who lacks compassion and feelings and has a tendency to become pompous and self-righteous.

THE SUIT OF CLUBS (PLATES 40–3)

Knave of Clubs

The Knave looks serenely to his left, gazing straight ahead towards the future. In both hands he is holding a heavy green, fertile club with buds bursting with new growth. The bare legs suggest a vulnerability (The Lover) but he wears blue shoes and his feet are well planted on the ground. Unlike the other three Knaves he is moving along a left-handed path and has flesh-coloured hair topped with a fillet-style red and yellow hat with a white headband. He carries with him a weighty wand of talent, ideas and youthful energy. He may possess the qualities of The King, but these are hidden behind the tunic and red mantle.

This young man has abounding talents and energies that need to be nurtured, developed and allowed to be expressed, otherwise they will be transmuted into disruptive, potentially harmful hyperactivity. The creative spirit must be given rein.

Knight of Clubs

The Knight is looking down in appreciation of the gifts, energies and talents that are embedded in the symbol of the gold-coloured Club held in his left hand. It is now a more manageable size, indicating the Knight has it under control. His horse (spirit) is also looking in the same direction but the Knight's body and mount are moving in the opposite direction. The simple, everyday fillet worn by the Knave is discarded for the lemniscate hat of The Magician, Force, the Knave and King of Money and the Knave of Swords. The well-decorated upper-body armour protects his heart and groin and the blue breeches and red hose are adorned with a yellow rosette; he wears a white shoe.

The horse's white body is hidden under a flesh-coloured blanket; its unbridled head suggests that the transformatory qualities of the Knight's spirit largely remain a secret (as in The High Priestess and The Empress). The blue mane reflects the blue hair found in The Pope, The Lover, The Hanged Man, Temperance, The Tower, The Star, The

Moon and Judgement as well as the Queen of Money.

This young person knows where he wants to be and understands how to capitalize on innate abilities. The Knight has the fire, energy and passion for creative works, and the intuitive ideas and flexibility of mind to progress in his quest for fulfilment.

In a negative mode he could become subversive and misdirect his talents.

Queen of Clubs

Her white tresses are as long and flowing as The Star and The World. She is looking down and to her left. The disproportionately large, top-heavy club – shaped more like a serious weapon – rests over her shoulder and nestles in her hand on her right thigh. Her left hand also gently rests on her other thigh. She sits comfortably with her legs apart on a throne that cannot be seen behind her voluminous red mantle, blue cotte with gold kirtle and girdle. Unlike the other three Queens, she is turned to her left and disregards the implement she is holding.

Abundant feminine energies tempered with love and guile, coupled with highly developed intuitive powers produce this formidable Queen who has boundless creativity and imaginative ideas. But, like the Knave and Knight, unless these abilities and energies are well directed and explored for positive ends, they could become overbearing and destructive.

King of Clubs

This young, beardless King looks serenely to the left (in the same direction as the Queen, Knight and Knave) and ahead into the future. His hat, with its half-hidden crown is a repeat of that worn by the King of Swords. He is also somewhat similarly dressed in well-decorated armour, red breeches, blue hose, red shoes and protective epaulettes. The gold armour belt protecting his solar plexus region draws attention to the area of 'gut feelings' (intuition). He is lightly balanced on his feet, sitting squarely on a throne that is somewhat similar to the throne of

Justice. In his right hand he holds a heavy white and gold mace in a non-threatening manner, while his left hand, like the Queen's, rests on his thigh or inner groin. He appears to be sitting in a relaxed posture, but this is deceptive because he is dressed and armed ready for action whenever necessary.

Through his balance and integration of the Masculine and Feminine Principles of rationality and intuition and his fertile imagination, creativity and high energy levels, he has the power and capability to manifest great benefits.

The single blue post to his throne indicates that he may err on the side of idealism rather than being a pragmatic ruler: this could lead him into unrealistic adventures or enterprises when, like the King of Cups, his heart may overrule his head. This King could become dangerous if he lacks discipline and his energies run out of control.

FAMILIARITY BREEDS COMPREHENSION

Deciphering the 78 Major and Minor Arcana cards tells us something about the cast of characters and influences in the story of our quest. Now, we can discover how their roles relate to each other in an apparently random, open-ended interaction which 'encodes' discrete messages so that we may understand where we are at present and the next step we need to take in the fulfilment of our quest.

As mentioned earlier, check that the deck you are using does have a consistent and bona fide symbolic language of vocabulary and logical grammar, otherwise the depth of meaning will be muddled and confusing.

For the serious aspirant, meditating on the symbols and symbolism of the deck can expand one's psychic awareness and intuition when using the cards for personal divination and for breaking down any negative, blocking constructs that separate us from who we really are. It is better for the reader to gain a general impression of the range of meanings and interpretations of each card rather than

attempting to memorize the whole deck. Let the intuition take over –
do not learn the meanings by rote. Without it sounding too 'New
Agey', it may help to become familiar with the Tarot and begin to
penetrate its depths of meaning if you turn over a new card each
morning from your randomly shuffled deck and hold the image and its
symbolism in your mind throughout the rest of the day.

6

ENCODING THE TAROT'S JOURNEY

The real voyage of discovery consists not in seeing new landscapes but in having fresh eyes.[1]

A s we have seen, layer upon layer of meaning can be revealed by the symbolism of each Tarot card. In reality, these cards are 78 'devices' to stimulate our innate knowingness and give us deep insights into our psyche, our thought patterns, our emotions and the stratagems we use to block our own 'path to freedom'. Freedom comes from having the courage to discover and know who we are. The Tarot has the potential to enable us to more readily recognize the driving power of the positive and negative forces within us, to become aware of how the confrontations of daily life are set up, and how we can move ahead on Life's Journey. It is a step-by-step plan, guide or map to show the way through our personal evolution, marking the pitfalls, trials and encounters that can direct our way forward. We all need help to open the shutters of the ego which conceal our true Higher Self.

The Tarot helps us to become aware of vague, half-forgotten or veiled thought patterns which may, if brought to the surface of the conscious mind, accelerate our journey and whatever else we may need to manifest in our lives. This implies an acceptance of responsibility for our own actions, and the fate that befalls us and all the people – for better or worse – we have encountered in our lives. In other words, is everything a matter of personal choice rather than good or bad luck?

Undoubtedly, some of us are afraid that, if we delve too deeply into our inner world, our complacency and current mindsets about our life and lifestyle may be seriously challenged. This may be why many people will have nothing to do with the cards, believing that the Tarot is dangerous and sinister, and possesses strange occult associations.

In his introduction to the book *Jung and Tarot: An Archetypal Journey*, Laurens van der Post wrote:

> [Jung] rated very highly all non-rational ways along which man in the past has tried to explore the mystery of life and stimulate man's conscious knowledge of the expanding universe around him into new areas of being and knowing. This is the explanation of his interest, for instance, in astrology and this, too, is the explanation of the significance of Tarot.
>
> He recognized at once, as he did in so many other games and primordial attempts at divination of the unseen and the future, that Tarot had its origin and anticipation in profound patterns of the collective unconscious with access to potentials of increased awareness uniquely at the disposal of these patterns.[2]

He went on to say:

> The unconscious and the conscious exist in a profound state of interdependence of each other and the well-being of one is impossible without the well-being of the other. If ever the connection between these two great states of being is diminished or impaired, man becomes sick and deprived of meaning ... consciousness for him is therefore not, as it is for instance for the logical positivists of our day, merely an intellectual and rational state of mind and spirit. It is not something which depends solely on man's capacity for articulation, as some schools of modern philosophy maintain to the point of claiming that that which cannot be articulated verbally and rationally is meaningless and not worthy of expression.[3]

When our attitude is receptive and non-judgemental and we allow ourselves to trust our own inner wisdom, the Tarot offers great insights to help us bring order out of chaos so that the choices we make will take us on to the next step of our quest.

The Tarot can give us the 'eyes to see' the signposts and milestones on our voyage of discovery – a path of initiation or rite of passage from the ego 'I' to the transcendent 'Self'. It is an occult system for contacting the inner knowingness of our subconscious mind, for drawing attention to our hidden fears and 'what makes us tick'; it tells us something about ourselves and what is happening at this moment in our lives. This can lead us to accept responsibility for our own actions and choices, and to realize that every choice we make has consequences that will be, to a minor or major extent, a factor that determines our future.

The question is whether we want to embark on this heroic journey or not. We must ask ourselves, 'Do I want/need to discover the truth and essence of who I am or should I be content to allow everything I do, think and feel be manipulated and controlled by the power of unconscious, irrational conditioning?' The Tarot presents us with the possible opportunities to take appropriate action by displaying to us – like a mirror – how we respond automatically to given circumstances.

Probably, most of us experienced our first encounter with the cards at a time when we were sufficiently intrigued by the idea that we might discover where and when something would happen or we would meet someone to transform our relationships, our finances, our luck, solve all our current problems and let us live happily ever after. Others may consult the Tarot when they are in a state of crisis or trauma, or they may want something/someone to help them make an important decision. For some it may be idle curiosity or simply seeking confirmation that what is happening in their lives is as they believe it should be.

Whatever the motive, we are drawn to the Tarot as we are to myths and fairy tales: we *know* that somehow they hold a fascinating key that will unlock a secret door, but we know not what it is we are about to enter.

There are three ways to read the cards:

   At an exoteric fortune-telling and prediction level

   At a mesoteric psychological level

   At an esoteric spiritual level

Almost without exception, the Tarot is read for fortune-telling and prediction. Many readers use the cards as a tool to aid their psychic abilities in much the same way as others use a crystal ball. Undoubtedly, some are highly gifted clairvoyants who may be able to predict certain future events or warn of impending troubles or good luck, but this misses the point of the Tarot's profound psychological and spiritual wisdom that can bring us to an awareness of what is going on in the here and now.

The second way accords with the Jungian transpersonal school of psychology's view that classical myths and fairy tales are archetypal expressions of human nature which can symbolically direct us toward *individuation*. Used in this context, the Reader can help the Querant to become aware of vague half-forgotten or discarded thought patterns which he or she may find incisive and uplifting and which open up a vision of how to create whatever they may be trying to manifest in their lives.

The third way is that of the Rudolf Steiner School, which tends to interpret myths and fairy tales as a portrayal of mystical soul experiences and cosmic spiritual truths and to interpret the Tarot as a pathway of transpersonal transformation. Here the Tarot is an oracle that can help us to transcend to a level where we are able to recognize our secret fears and the powerful unconscious forces that control the choices we make and which significantly influence our future endeavours and fulfilment.

The Tarot can and will introduce us to the 'tall, dark strangers' who are very much alive in the deep recesses of the shadows of the mind. Once met, understood, acknowledged and loved, these 'dark strangers' will indeed transform our lives because they are our true 'soul mates'. But until we identify, accept and fully realize these characters within, it is unlikely that we will be attracted to a real, live 'soul mate'. It is more the case that we have already met such living persons within our social orbit, but because of our lack of awareness we were unable to recognize their presence. Helping us to come to terms with these shadow figures is a way of using a Tarot reading to bring insights and a self-understanding to our attitudes and mindsets or whatever else may be blocking the way forward.

In chapter 2 we had our first brief glimpse of the story told by the Tarot. Since then we have become familiar with the enigmatic language of the symbolism shrouded in the pictographs, the suits and numbers of the cards, and now we can understand the vocabulary and grammar of that language. In our quest for self-knowledge we shall see how the 21 Major Arcana cards translate into a graphic map of the sequences of the archetypal, mythical journey in three segments: the Hero's/Heroine's Call to Adventure, the Initiation and the Return. Their story begins in a dark forest at the foot of a mountain. They follow a winding path through the dense trees and undergrowth but gradually it gets lighter until, eventually, at the summit, they can see the blue skies and breathe the clear air.

The 'map' of their journey becomes clearer when the 21 cards are set out in a numerical sequence in three rows of seven cards each as shown below in figure 23. Each card is a marker along the path that The Fool – each one of us – must follow, step by step, on the way to illumination and self-knowledge and the fulfilment of our own, individual destiny.

Figure 23: The Journey Through the Major Arcana

Line 1   **1** THE MAGICIAN   **2** THE HIGH PRIESTESS **3** THE EMPRESS

Line 2   **8** JUSTICE   **9** THE HERMIT   **10** THE WHEEL OF FO

Line 3   **15** THE DEVIL   **16** THE TOWER OF   **17** THE STAR
                                           DESTRUCTION

4 THE EMPEROR   **5** THE POPE   **6** THE LOVER   **7** THE CHARIOT

11 FORCE   **12** THE HANGED MAN   **13** DEATH   **14** TEMPERANCE

18 THE MOON   **19** THE SUN   **20** JUDGEMENT   **21** THE WORLD

OUR STORY BEGINS

The Call to Adventure

The first step on the path is marked by The Magician who personifies our infinite potentialities, our instinctive appreciation of the Earth energies and our ability to thrive in the material world. We feel invincible and without fully understanding why, we respond to the Call to Adventure – after all, this is what Heroes and Heroines do!

We next encounter The High Priestess (the archetypal virgin) who introduces the dimensions of the invisible realms of the spirit and spiritual teachings followed by The Empress who expresses the Feminine Principle of intuition and the full spectrum of love and sensuality before we move ahead to experience The Emperor's sense of logic and rationality that epitomizes the Masculine Principle. These three embody the archetypal, cosmic Woman and Man.

Next we come into contact with The Pope's world of order, discipline, spiritual tenets, sacred traditions and institutions that lead us to The Lover's all-too-human experience of longing and yearning for love and contentment but, in our heart, we know we are now standing at a crossroads. Here the decision is whether to retreat or proceed. If we follow our innate sense we will mount The Chariot, drawn by the psyche and life force, to take us along an unknown, unfamiliar and even uncomfortable course.

These first seven step-by-step teachings and disciplines mark the neophyte Hero/Heroine's *call to adventure*, but we need to bear in mind that any negative resistance will block the way forward.

At the very beginning of the journey The Magician warns of the danger that if we misuse our natural gifts to create a deceitful 'magic' we can become cheats, con artists or illusionists. In turn, The High Priestess can become a controlling fortune teller and witch; The Empress can become a temptress and a hedonist, lusting after sex without love; The Emperor can become a tyrant and an abuser of power, bringing about a lack of self-control; The Pope, a dogmatic martinet and punisher; The Lover, a seducer, emotionally unstable and confused victim of indecision and idleness; and if the Charioteer feels he or she must tightly hold onto the reins and lacks the inner courage for the adventure of self-discovery then the journey will have to be abandoned. We need to overcome the hazards, spurn negative temptations to abuse power and begin to understand what we have to do next to discover more about our own psychological make-up, our anxieties, conditioning and need to control.

The Initiation

These next seven steps begin with Justice, which tells us about introducing balance into our lives and accepting responsibilities instead of seeking excuses by projecting blame onto others. The Hermit's solitude and introspection will help us to achieve a deeper self-understanding to find the inner light to illuminate any tendency to be self-centred or unable to form relationships with others – and ourselves! Through meditation and contemplation we can glimpse aspects of our inner wisdom and acknowledge the human desire to satisfy a spiritual need. With such inner light comes the vision to view positively the hand Fate has dealt us on The Wheel of Fortune. This step is an opportunity to experience naturally changing rhythms and circumstances. Here we also learn to accept whatever good or bad 'luck' may befall us and to treat *an accident as an adventure misunderstood*. Alternatively, we can drown ourself in sorrow and self-pity, or even perversely believe we do not even deserve whatever good fortune Fate has bestowed upon us. Although to our naïve state of mind there appears to be an inexorable life force over which we have no control, the process of self-discovery gives us the free will to change our state of mind.

We have now arrived at the critical midway point of our journey. Here we meet Force and, by a strange alchemical process, we must summon up the strength to go into the depths of our *shadow*. This marks a significant turning point when we will need the courage and fortitude to emulate Theseus and go down into the dark secret tunnels of our unconscious mind and enter the labyrinth to confront our inner monsters, come to terms with the *shadow* and then begin the ascent to the Light of Consciousness. If at this point we decide to continue the journey – to become a *man* or *woman of knowledge* – there will be no room for weak excuses or lax behaviour. It is a time to recognize our human frailties and, like The Hanged Man, we may well find our world has turned upside down.

Whilst still hanging helplessly strung up, immobilized and 'stuck' in an unfamiliar environment, we may experience despair, inner dread and fear, knowing that the next step along the path demands that we 'suffer' a death – a psychological death if you will – before we can be reborn on a higher plane.

From now on, nothing will be quite the same: our foibles, prejudices, irrational thinking and motivations will come under close scrutiny. Time is needed to reflect, reassess and prepare for another step forward into the unknown, transformatory realm of the thirteenth card Death.

These last three cards are sequential tests of our resolve to overcome a fear of the radical changes inevitably triggered by the awakening of self-understanding and freedom from the compulsion of our unconscious forces. They prepare us to meet Temperance.

When Temperance appears, our life energies begin to flow again. Having successfully undergone the trials of this second octave, which began with Justice, we now feel the presence of our heaven-sent inner guides. Whilst this staging post marks the attainment of clarity, Castaneda warns us that *clarity* is also fraught with the danger of believing in our own invincibility. We must therefore ensure that the power of the alchemical elixir flowing between Temperance's two chalices is never used for evil or unscrupulous purposes.

The Return

The Devil, the fifteenth card, is a milestone that marks the preparatory work for the final and most hazardous phase of the journey. How might we use or misuse our newly acquired power of clarity of mind? Here we can be trapped into becoming manipulative and self-centred, but our apparent sense of invincibility is The Devil's way of hiding our self-doubts and fears. Here we must repulse the self-centredness and ego-building talents of The Devil and trust the very essence of our being. On the other hand, provided we do not retreat from our inner resolve to proceed, The Devil – in the guise of Lucifer – is the bringer of light and illumination.

The Tower of Destruction is the next step marking a breakdown or loss of the 'I', the ego-self, and a reminder that 'the higher we climb, the harder we fall' from the perch of pride and superiority. A sense of humbleness and acceptance is demanded before we can proceed on the final stages of our quest and take a step forward on the path of love.

The Star shows us how to become self-nurturing; how to use our intuition and psychic abilities to be in tune with nature, care for others and the Planet, to avoid polluting the Earth, to tread lightly and to have a wider, universal view of what is happening around us. The Moon, personifying the Feminine Principle, reinforces our understanding of the natural forces and a sense of the rhythms of life and living. However, we must beware of engaging in 'the dark side' and misusing our basic instincts. This is the final test: will we succumb to the temptation to engage in the forces of darkness, or will we choose to proceed towards the light?

When The Sun casts its light on The Moon, we emerge from the *shadow* to express our true self with 'nothing to hide'. This creates an aura of the power of love; but, yet again, we must beware that this newly found brightness in our life does not overpower others.

Judgement marks the step when rebirth takes place, when we can begin to live by grace, discernment and humility. Finally, we arrive at the place of fulfilment and self-realization where we are at one with The World in a state of joyous transformation, thus completing the full circle from naivety to become the evolved, mature Magician of wisdom. Although we are no longer in thrall of our *shadow*, we must beware of 'resting on our laurels' because the Hero's journey never ends.

Where or when does The Fool – ourselves – impede or assist us on our travels? It is for each one of us to decide in the first instance whether to even embark on the journey and, having done so, to what extent we may deviate from the path, accelerate, slow down or even stop completely at any one point. It is The Fool who either succumbs to fear, turns to the misuse of power, or has the resolve, commitment, tenacity and courage to press ahead. The Fool expresses the infinite spectrum of human nature and reminds us – warns us – not to waste precious time in idleness or prevarication.

Horizontal line One: The Magician to The Chariot

This line concerns the *material world*.

This is the phase of the neophyte Hero/Heroine's period for instruction from the archetypal perfect Women (cards II and III) and perfect Men (cards IIII and V) and for understanding how they influence the choices we make. The turning point occurs when the Charioteer takes courage and decides to embark upon an unknown path to an unknown destination.

Horizontal line Two: Justice to Temperance

This line concerns the *psychological world*.

It takes courage to delve deeper into aspects of the mind, our individual psychology, character and make-up, in order to experience Earthly realities and encounter ego-consciousness, but this undertaking culminates in an awakening of the alchemical processes and the power of self-awareness.

Horizontal line Three: The Devil to The World

This line concerns the *psycho/spiritual world*.

When the strong temptations to misuse our power for evil and destruction (cards XV, XVI and XVIII) are resisted the great works on the path of transformation finally reach completion.

These three horizontal lines are summarized in the following table.

Cards I to VII	The line of the exoteric realm of the gods and the archetypes	Body and Learning
Cards VIII to XIIII	The line of the mesoteric realm of illumination and psyche	Mind and Clarity
Cards XV to XXI	The line of the esoteric realm of self-realization and the spirit	Discipline and Power

Table 2: The Three Stages of the Journey Through the Major Arcana

In chapter 3, The Language of the Tarot, it was emphasized that the Tarot must follow the usual conventions or rules inherent in any language, including the way it is written and read. English is written and read from left to right, Arabic from right to left, and Japanese from top right down to bottom left. However, this is where the Tarot breaks such conventions. As we have seen above, the cards are read from left to right, but an additional and greater depth of meaning can be revealed when the vertical lines of cards are also read from top to bottom.

The cards along the top line mark the progression through the initiations set by the archetypes. The topmost card in each vertical line tells us what is or could be manifested in our lives, and the card in the middle row of the line tells us what must be done to achieve a positive outcome in relation to the card on the bottom row. If the needs of the middle card are not met, the card on the bottom line will remain in the *shadow* and retard or prevent further progress. The following examples suggest ways in which the top card is moderated by the card in the middle row, thus creating the necessary balance to facilitate a positive outcome for the bottom card, after which we are able to progress to the top card in the next vertical line.

Vertical Line One

This line concerns our *inherent characteristics* and *human nature*.

> **Magician** – our innate characteristics and potential
> **Justice** – integrity and moral understanding
> **The Devil** – the *shadow* is self-doubt, misuse of natural gifts,
> and naivety

The Magician is clever and has infinite potential, but without the balance and discernment of Justice he could succumb to the *shadow* figure in The Devil and become a manipulative trickster and cheat.

Vertical Line Two

This line concerns *insight* and *self-awareness*.

> **The High Priestess** – the archetypal virgin
> **The Hermit** – seeing one's inner light
> **The Tower of Destruction** – the *shadow* is self-destruction
> and misuse of occult power

The High Priestess expresses the need to be independent and reflective, to explore the occult ('hidden') realms and to find oneself through introspection (The Hermit). However, The Tower of Destruction tells us we must beware of becoming self-indulgent, egotistical and over-confident.

Vertical Line Three

This line concerns *intuition* and *replenishment*.

> **The Empress** – the archetypal mother and
> Aphrodite/Venus
> **The Wheel of Fortune** – Fate
> **The Star** – the *shadow* is greed and self-centredness

Through The Empress (the Feminine Principle and intuition) we can understand and accept the ever-changing cycles and rhythms of the tangible world. The Wheel Of Fortune reminds us of the uncertainty and changes of life, but this can be balanced by the essence of The Star when we nurture ourselves, humanity and Nature.

Vertical Line Four

This line concerns *instinctiveness* and *clarity of mind*.

> **The Emperor** – the archetypal father
> **Force** – the quest for self-understanding
> **The Moon** – the *shadow* is misuse of power and self-delusion

The Emperor expresses the instinctive Masculine Principle, worldly power, self-assertion and rationality, but these characteristics need to be tempered by Force, which demands a high degree of self-knowledge if we are to avoid The Moon's tendency for illusion and self-aggrandizement.

Vertical Line Five

This line concerns *introspection* and *moral attitudes*.

> **The Pope** – the archetypal wise man
> **The Hanged Man** – time for contemplation and
>   introspection
> **The Sun** – the shadow is selfish thoughtlessness and
>   egocentricity

The Pope represents tradition, respect, integrity and spiritual wisdom. This requires deep contemplation and a time for reflection on these profound matters (The Hanged Man) before we can become fully realized (The Sun) and express our relationship with the world at large.

Vertical Line Six

This line concerns *indecision* and *rebirth*.

> **The Lover** – time for making choices and creativity
> **Death** – transformation
> **Judgement** – the *shadow* is tyrannical weakness, lack of
> commitment, permanent confusion and stultified
> creativity

The Lover is in a state of indecision and wants to please everyone but ends up pleasing no one, not even himself. He is in danger of becoming caught up in an eternal triangle or 'going round in circles' due to the confusion created by his egocentricities. He must therefore experience the psychological Death of his present state of immaturity before he can be reborn (Judgement) on a higher plane of consciousness.

Vertical Line Seven

This line concerns *independence* and *celebration*.

> **The Chariot** – the courage to follow one's
> intuition / instincts
> **Temperance** – the alchemical blend of life's energies
> **The World** – the *shadow* is fear of life and regret

Trusting only in his intuition and instinct, the Charioteer has the courage to journey into the unknown and to be transported onto another plane where the angelic Temperance will guide him towards the fulfilment of his quest, which is to experience The World's gifts of the elixir of life and to dance to the music of the Universe.

Although we are The Fool, Providence has presented us with a chart (figure 23) which will guide us through the 21 milestones of the magical quest to discover the secret treasure trove that is the essence of our being. Of course, a map is only an approximate two-dimensional representation. It is only when we set forth that we encounter the hurdles, hazards and obstacles of the actual terrain, but we can prepare for the *call to adventure* by studying the signs and symbols encoded in the cards. As The Fool, we must be alert to misreading the map due to our own foolishness – our naivety – and beware of the myriad diversions and false directions set up by the events and encounters presented by the Minor Arcana cards. All voyagers who journey into unknown territory use a compass, sextant or satellite to make periodic checks on their position. A random spread reading of the Tarot cards serves the same purpose: to give an insight on our present position and thus bring the immediate situation/circumstances into focus at a conscious level. As we gradually navigate our way towards our destination, we will emerge from the shadows to come face to face with ourselves!

7

READING A SPREAD

cceptance of the workings and efficacy of the Tarot is no less a matter of leaping the credibility gap than the general acceptance of current physics concerning time, space, random chance, the unseen worlds of other realities and the oneness of the Universe. The theory of chaos clearly indicates that there is no chance randomness in the natural world and that nature has a mysterious organizing power.

However, many people remain uncertain about, even hostile to anything that smacks of the paranormal, which is not surprising when we take into account the number of spurious fortune tellers who trade in predicting future events. Science may debunk extra-sensory perception (ESP), but in an article in *The Sunday Telegraph* Science File: 'Making sense of ESP', Robert Matthews sees a brighter future for mystics and clairvoyants. Robert Matthews reported on the scientist Professor Robert Morris, who took the Koestler Chair in Parapsychology at Edinburgh University from 1985 to 1998:

> According to Professor Morris, evidence is mounting that extra-sensory perception (ESP) such as clairvoyance is a genuine – but feeble – phenomenon. It also appears that it is possible to boost one's ESP abilities … [and that such abilities] lie within the known laws of science. He suspects that [clairvoyants] may be sensitive to subtle sources of information in ways they cannot articulate, and that these provide cues that give the impression of clairvoyance.[1]

Throughout the World, many people resort to some form of divination to resolve a major predicament or simply to decide where and when to go on holiday, and so it may not come as a surprise to learn that there are many people who 'consult' the cards on a daily basis. This may be thought of as an over-dependency but in our Western culture it is not always easy to contact our inner knowingness because we are conditioned to rely on logic and intellectual argument rather than reaching down from the head to the heart and trusting one's 'gut feeling'.

Instead of spreading a deck of Tarot cards, casting the I Ching's yarrow sticks or consulting an astrologer, some people use dowsing rods or a pendulum while others may turn to prayer to invoke 'guidance from above'. Whatever the chosen system or tool, it can help us to get in touch with our intuition.

The Tarot is a sacred treasure house of knowledge, universal truths and wisdom: the 78 cards can tell us all we need to understand about human nature, the human condition and how we tend to respond to the daily and yearly round of events and circumstances. Many folk are sceptical of such a claim, and the process of shuffling that randomly selects a small number of cards from the whole Major and Minor Arcana deck only serves to reinforce their scepticism. We should bear in mind that other great divinatory systems for self-understanding, such as the I Ching, also depend on a system of random selection. Of course, much depends on the understanding, interpretation and intuitive experience of the Tarot Reader, but another significant factor is how the Querant 'hears' and interprets what is being said by the Reader.

People often contact me after a broadcast on Tarot readings, or after reading something I have written or listening to the tape recording of their Tarot reading, to tell me that what I have said has had a special significance for them. Often this can be puzzling because I know, after re-reading the article or listening again to the broadcast tape, that I had most definitely not said what they thought I had said: it was their interpretation that was all important to them.

In a theatre, there may be 500 or more people in the audience of, say, a Shakespeare play in which, incidentally, the director has already cast his or her 'slant' on the Bard's words. It is said that the inherent genius of Shakespeare is that his plays have a universal appeal at three different levels: whether a member of the audience is an earthy, bawdy peasant-like character, conscious only of the material (exoteric) world; or is a merchant, artisan or intellectual type who may have experienced the occult (mesoteric) world; or is a person who has an understanding and knowledge of the mystical, spiritual (esoteric) world. Everyone in an audience hears the same words and sees the same action on stage, but how each person is influenced, touched and intellectually and emotionally affected is dependent upon whatever is pertinent to each individual at a given moment or period in their life. Sometimes a subtle nuance or the powerful impact of the whole drama can produce a spark of insight or even a lightning flash that takes that person a step closer to self-realization. Whether we are looking at a play or film, reading a book, viewing a painting or simply hearing what a child or adult is saying, the experience can trigger something that will be significant to one particular person whereas the stimulus may create totally different meanings and responses for others. These personal responses are more to do with individual intuitive insights rather than our critical, intellectual capabilities.

When we let our intuitive, subconscious mind listen, the images and words can facilitate the process for us to recognize a way forward. Energy follows thought and, depending upon willpower, tenacity and commitment, our thoughts, aspirations and hoped-for outcomes can either become realized and manifested or float around in the ether and never come to anything. Perhaps we allow these thoughts to languish at the back of our minds as 'wishful thinking' because we are afraid of the possible consequences if they were to materialize. Sometimes, a Tarot reading can facilitate these thought patterns to rise up to the surface of the mind and be looked at from a positive viewpoint. By facing up to his or her fears the Querant may be able to turn those unexplored longings into beneficial changes.

Whether a Querant has a serious dilemma over career, moving house or a partnership matter, or just light-heartedly hopes for some good and exciting news to break the monotony of their current situation, the Reader's task is to act as a guide to shed some light on what is happening in the immediate *present* which may lead to finding a way forward. It is not the Reader's job to predict, or even suggest to the Querant what he or she should do. A Reader's responsibility is to act as a neutral facilitator to allow the Querant's aspirations to emerge through their own innate wisdom. Plato held the view that we are all gifted with total wisdom and knowledge; the task of a teacher – or Tarot Reader – is to help us to *remember*!

The Tarot Reader's psychic, clairvoyant or ESP abilities will, no doubt, come into play, but it is essential that any preconceptions about the Querant are abandoned and, of course, the cards are correctly interpreted. In other words, the Reader's task as a neutral facilitator is to interpret the cards as they appear.

All our outward manifestations – what we do, what we think, our belief systems and how we act – are generated by the inner, unknown forces. Through the Tarot, the more we can illuminate the dark recesses of the *shadow*, the greater our freedom.

THE READING

Your Tarot deck should always be treated with care and respect and should be protected, since it is a means of accessing sacred wisdom and universal truths. In accordance with tradition, the cards should be kept wrapped in a piece of fine natural silk which, when laid flat, is large enough for a full 21-card spread to be laid out with space to place the remaining cards while the reading takes place. The cards should only be handled by you except when reading for a Querant. From time to time, depending on how often the cards are used, they should be wiped with a damp soft cloth and warm water to clean away any negative energies that may have accumulated.

Let us assume you are about to read the cards. Beforehand, you might need to go through a short ritual, such as a few minutes of meditation to clear your mind of all preconceptions and create an empathy with the Querant, and do the same if you are reading a spread for yourself. Finally, ensure none of the cards are reversed before the pack is shuffled.

The Querant should sit beside you, on your left (or on your right if you are left-handed). In this position you are both together in resonance – on the same side as each other – otherwise, if the Querant is sitting opposite it creates a polarity between you. Moreover, they can only see the spread upside down.

If the Querant is not familiar with a Tarot deck, explain in brief, general terms the meaning of the Court cards, the numbers and the suits, and that the Major cards indicate the milestones or steps along life's path. Invite the Querant to focus attention on whatever may be their issue at hand. You do not want them to tell you what the issue is but ask them to hold it in mind while they are shuffling the cards.

Before reading the spread, advise the Querant that if they feel the reading is off course or tangential to their main issue they must tell you as you are there to help to focus on the nub of the matter that is their particular concern. Some Querants will discuss their issue as the reading progresses; others are determined to keep silent until the session has ended.

Hand the deck to the Querant, who should thoroughly shuffle the cards (to put his or her own energies into the pack) and then ask the Querant to cut the deck into three piles with the left hand (right hand if left-handed) and put the three piles together again in a different order. Repeat the process twice more and finally place the deck face down on the silk cloth. This is known as *mixing the elements of the outer world*.

Reversed Cards

Sometimes during the shuffling one or more cards may fall out and the Querant will inadvertently put them back the wrong way up in a 'reversed' or 'upside-down' order. Other Querants, who are used to handling cards, may split them like a professional card player which, inevitably, reverses about half the pack. On other occasions the whole spread may be reversed simply because the Querant has handed the cards back to the Reader that way round. Some Readers never, or hardly ever, go through their deck to change all the reversed cards into an upright position. I believe this can lead to a spread being interpreted in a falsely negative manner and recommend that all the cards are checked and placed 'upright' before handing the pack to the Querant.

How should we interpret a card or cards that are 'reversed'? Many Readers tend to read the meaning of a reversed a card as being directly opposite to its positive value. For example, a reversed Three of Cups might imply that the Querant is unsettled, feeling discontented or wasting emotional energies on a lost cause or affairs of the heart. Again, if Justice is reversed it could mean that the Querant is experiencing an imbalance in their life or a degree of unfairness. However, for a fortune teller, a reversed Justice might predict an unexpected or poor outcome of a legal matter such as a divorce settlement. Some Readers interpret a reversed card as a mere warning rather than predicting some dire consequence.

If you, as the Tarot Reader, believe in the principles of 'serendipity' (the faculty of making fortunate and unexpected discoveries by accident) and 'synchronicity' (Jung's view that a 'coincidence' may have a significant or meaningful link), the meaning or interpretation would be modified when a card is reversed, provided that the Reader handed the deck to the Querant with no cards reversed. Whether a card is reversed or not, embedded in each one is a degree of antithesis: the positive or negative 'value' or significance of a card will be determined by the surrounding cards in the spread. Sometimes, a spread can communicate how an issue could be resolved by transforming – reversing – conflict into cooperation.

One final point concerning the Minor Arcana suits: excluding the Court cards, all the Money cards and all the Clubs (except the Ace) are the same pattern whichever way up they appear; all the Cups and Swords are either up or down with the exception of Swords numbers Two and Eight.

Laying out a Spread

When the cards are well shuffled, take the pack from the Querant and lay out the 21-card spread as described below. Always keep the spread and the remaining cards on the silk cloth.

Lay out the cards in three rows of seven cards each, working from left to right, as in figure 24. Allow time for the Querant to view the spread before you begin.

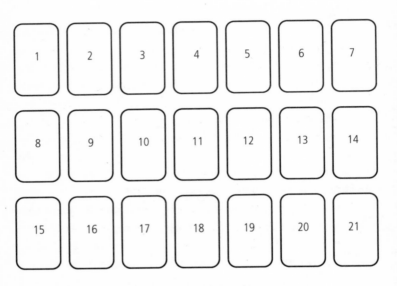

Figure 24: The 21-Card Spread Layout

The reading

The significance/interpretation of any card may be modified by its location in the spread, on which line it occurs, the adjacent cards and whether it is at the beginning, middle or near the end of the line.

Before we go on to study examples of actual readings, it is important to understand the basic principles involved in giving a reading. These are outlined in the Six Steps given below. (If you have a Tarot deck, you can lay out a spread while following the Six Steps.)

Step One: *The Significator*

Focus on the card in the centre of the middle row: this is known as *The Significator*. It falls on the space number eleven. The card in a spread that lands on this position usually signifies the Querant's issue at hand and the crux of a matter or a turning point. More often than not, it is the principle reason why the Querant has come for a reading.

Step Two: *Review the number of Major Arcana cards in the spread*

Due to the ratio of Major to Minor cards in the pack, on average there will be six or seven Majors in any one spread.

Point out the number of Major Arcana cards and in broad terms, draw attention to their significance in the spread.

Step Three: *Review the predominance of any one or more suits and note whether any of the Court or numbered cards bear the same value*

Draw the Querant's attention to such predominance and similarities and discuss their specific meaning.

These first three Steps are a summary to help both the Querant and the Reader to feel the general direction the reading is taking. At this point the Reader should not encourage the Querant to discuss any issues so as to avoid preconceived views that might influence the reading. On the other hand, the Querant should be given the opportunity to discuss the reading, especially if he/she believes it is off the mark. At this stage the Reader will want to review the reading thus far.

Step Four: *Read the eight cards surrounding the Significator*

These cards should be read in the following order:

Line 1	place numbers 4, 11, 18
Line 2	place numbers 10, 11, 12
Line 3	place numbers 3, 11, 19
Line 4	place numbers 5, 11, 17

The cards – numbers 3, 4, 5, 10, 12, 17, 18, 19 – surrounding card 11 will expand the overall picture, and reading the four lines will give a broad synopsis of the Querant's main issue.

Step Five: *Read the three horizontal rows*

The top seven cards (numbers 1 to 7) are the realm of the exoteric, day-to-day life and living and may represent long-term or current issues or possible conflicts.

The middle row of cards (numbers 8 to 14) represents the mesoteric realm and concerns our attitudes and mindsets that can determine possible outcomes.

The bottom row of cards (numbers 15 to 21) is the esoteric (spiritual) realm where the Querant's issue may be resolved. Often, simply through a process of self-acceptance and forgiveness of oneself or others, this line indicates what needs to be raised to a conscious level.

Step Six: *Read the vertical lines*

The interpretation of each line is governed by a key word based on the symbolic meaning of the numbers 1 to 7 and related to the top line of the 21-card spread of the Major Arcana cards (*see* figure 23 and pages 118–19). The key words, each of which begins with the letter 'I', are accompanied by additional 'buzz' words and questions to amplify the interpretation. Of course, the key words given here are only a suggestion – it is for every Reader to develop their own preferred key words for each line.

Line One (Place numbers 1, 8, 15)
KEY WORD: Inherent Characteristics

I – the Self

Infinite potentiality

ANTITHESIS:

The *shadow*

Self-deception

Is there a hidden agenda or some ulterior motive that may bring confusion or deceit into the equation?

Line Two (Place numbers 2, 9, 16)
KEY WORD: Insight

The invisible worlds

Self-awareness

Inner secrets

The core of one's being

ANTITHESIS

Separation (confrontation)

Longing

Is there a degree of manipulation or secrecy that clouds
the issue?

Line Three (Place numbers 3, 10,17)
KEY WORD: Intuition

The Feminine Principle

Reconciliation

Sensuality

Replenishment and renewal

ANTITHESIS

Is there a need to be more self-nurturing, nourishing and
sensuous, and acknowledge the changing rhythms and cycles
of life?

Line Four (Place numbers 4, 11, 18)
KEY WORD: Instinct

The Masculine Principle

The material world

Setting boundaries

Clarity of mind

Leadership

ANTITHESIS

Danger of illusion

The issue demands rationality and clarity of mind to avoid
self-delusion; have boundaries been set?

Line Five (Place numbers 5, 12, 19)

KEY WORD: Introspection

  Self-discipline

  Conscience

  Responsibilities

  Order

  Compassion

  Personal values and what we need to learn

ANTITHESIS

Does the issue require order, discipline, and time for thoughtful contemplation without over-assertiveness?

Line Six (Place numbers 6, 13, 20)

KEY WORD: Indecision

  Making choices

  Creativity

  Human consciousness

  The inner voice

ANTITHESIS

If there is indecision, is it because of a fear of changing circumstances?

Line Seven (Place numbers 7, 14, 21)

KEY WORD: Independence

  The quest

  The cycles of change

  Illumination

  Courage to journey into the unknown

  Fulfilment

  Completion

ANTITHESIS

Can we 'Let go of the reins' (controlling tendencies) and allow intuition and instinct to lead to an unknown destination where the outcome may result in fulfilment and freedom?

Step Seven: *Conclude the reading*

Before bringing the reading to a close, invite questions to ensure that the Querant feels the reading is complete. He or she may want to know more about a particular card or would like further clarification on a specific aspect of the reading.

If there are unanswered questions it may be appropriate to lay out a new five-card spread. (Again, you do not want to know the nature of the Querant's question.) Gather up the 21 cards and randomly insert these into the main pack; alternatively, use the 57 unused cards. Ask the Querant to shuffle the pack as before and lay out a spread in a 'V' formation with two cards on each arm of the V and one at the point (*see* figure 25). Cards one and two set up the issue, card three is the tipping point indicating how the circumstances may change and cards four and five suggest a likely course of action to resolve the matter. Sometimes, it can be helpful to openly discuss the reading.

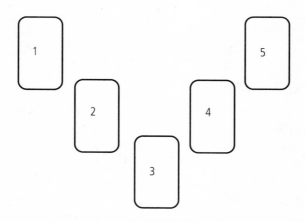

Figure 25: The Five-Card Spread

Many other forms of spreads will be found in various books on the Tarot, but I believe the uncomplicated 21-card spread comprehensively deals with all circumstances.

How Often is it Appropriate to Consult the Cards?

Unless you are either a professional Tarot Reader or one of the exceptional few who feel unable to get out of bed in the mornings before the cards have been shuffled and spread for a ritual daily reading, the majority of us probably only take out the cards from the package or silk wrapping no more than two or three times a year. Often, either reading for ourselves or visiting a Tarot Reader is only prompted when we are faced with a dilemma or feel the need for guidance to resolve a situation where we do not know which way to turn. At these times of stress or trauma, a Tarot reading can indeed bring clarity and guidance to get us 'back on track'.

EXAMPLES OF READING A SPREAD

The following examples for David and Zoe are intended to illustrate how to put a reading into practice. A reading session usually takes about an hour and a half and so these examples will only bring out the salient points – the 'bare bones' if you will – without putting too much 'flesh' on the outline skeleton.

Example Reading One: David

This reading was for a businessman in his mid-fifties who will be referred to as David. He was casually well-dressed and self-assured. His 'issue' was not discussed before the reading. Below is the layout of his spread:

Step One: *The Significator*
In all my readings I have never ceased to be surprised that, by serendipity, the card that turns up in a spread in space number 11 invariably indicates a Querant's main or associated issue.

In this reading, the Significator card in the centre space Number 11 is The Lover. This Major Arcana card suggests David's issue is about being faced with making important decisions, choosing which direction to take and how and where to focus his creative energies.

The presence of The Emperor, the King of Money and the two Aces suggest that David is likely to be a man who is comfortable in the material world and his issue concerns business activities rather than personal relationships.

Step Two: *Reviewing the number of Major Arcana cards in the spread*
There are five Major cards in the spread:

IV The Emperor	materiality and the material world
V The Pope	a quest to satisfy essential core values and principles
VI The Lover	making important decisions
VII The Chariot	entering unknown territory
XIII Death	making/accepting significant changes

It is interesting to note that the first four cards appear in the same sequence as they occur in the Tarot deck.

Step Three: *Reviewing the predominance of any one or more suits and any cards bearing the same numbers*

Ace, 4, 5, 7 and Queen of Cups	David is a man who relies on his emotions and intuition to guide him in his dealings.
2, 3, 4 and 10 of Swords	David is a gifted man who knows how to live on his wits
Ace, 8 and 10 of Clubs	indicate an abundance of energy and imagination
3, Knight and King of Money	David is well grounded in the material world

Line 1   **1** KING OF MONEY   **2** TEN OF CLUBS   **3** ACE OF CUPS

Line 2   **8** ACE OF CLUBS   **9** FOUR OF SWORDS   **10** FIVE OF CUPS

Line 3   **15** THREE OF SWORDS **16** DEATH   **17** TEN OF SWORDS

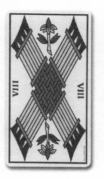

4 SEVEN OF CUPS   **5** QUEEN OF CUPS   **6** EIGHT OF CLUBS   **7** KNIGHT OF MONEY

11 THE LOVER   **12** THE CHARIOT   **13** THREE OF MONEY   **14** TWO OF CLUBS

18 FOUR OF CUPS   **19** TWO OF SWORDS   **20** THE EMPEROR   **21** THE POPE

The Aces reinforce the impression that he is well gifted. The two number tens – Clubs and Swords – indicate he may be on a threshold and that if he allows the relevant changes to happen in his life they could lift him to a higher level.

These first three Steps are a summary of the spread to help both the Querant and the Reader to 'feel' the general direction the reading is taking. At this stage it also offers the Querant the opportunity to comment on the Reader's interpretation of the main grouping of the cards before going into the detailed reading.

Step Four: *Reading the eight cards surrounding the Significator*

Line One	place numbers 4, 11, 18
Line Two	place numbers 10, 11, 12
Line Three	place numbers 3, 11, 19
Line Four	place numbers 5, 11, 17

These four lines will give a broad synopsis of David's main issue and the direction the reading will take.

Line One: David's current dreams and aspirations (Four of Cups) are causing a restlessness and sense of uncertainty (Seven of Cups). He appears to be at a crossroads (The Lover), knowing that whatever particular direction he chooses it could have far-reaching consequences affecting the life and lifestyle of both himself and his family.

Line Two: Whatever aspirations may be at the back of his mind, any change in direction will need to be allied to working with a more altruistic sense of purpose rather than simply to satisfy a material gain (Five of Cups). To achieve such a goal, David must have the courage of his convictions and go where his heart takes him into uncharted territory (The Chariot).

Line Three: There appears to be a conflict: he is in two minds (Two of Swords) about where his heart (Ace of Cups) could lead him.

Line Four: Changes in direction heralded by The Lover could allow ideas and ambitions to be explored that could have intellectually satisfying consequences (Ten of Swords) that David would also find emotionally fulfilling (Queen of Cups).

Step Five: *Reading the three horizontal lines*
The top line (place numbers 1 to 7) tells us where David is now, in the material world.

The middle line (place numbers 8 to 14) tells us something about what matters/issues are currently occupying his thoughts.

The bottom line (place numbers 15 to 21) tells us what may be his aspirations, his unexpressed ideas and perhaps where he would like to be heading.

The Top Line: Here we see a man of substance. He knows he has reached the end of a cycle (Ten and Eight of Clubs). A decision to move on may refocus and recharge his energies onto some new activity that will give him a deeper sense of pleasure (the cards of Cups) as well as satisfying his financial needs (King and Knight of Money) and his innate zest for life.

The Middle Line: How can David harness his unbounded energies and creative talents (Ace of Clubs) in a way that will bring him satisfaction (Four of Swords) and be of benefit to other people (Five of Cups)? The Lover and The Chariot call on him to allow Providence to guide him in his choice of direction and to embark on some new venture that could result in comforts and benefits (Three of Money) for other people as well as for himself, but the outcome may still not be as stimulating as he would like (Two of Clubs).

The Bottom Line: David is searching for intellectual challenges that he would find emotionally and financially rewarding (Three of Swords) but to achieve this, his current activities may need a transformational change (Death). This might not only be uplifting (Ten of Swords) but may also create the circumstances in which his aspirations could be realized (Four of Cups). But at the moment he is finding it difficult to be decisive (Two of Swords).

The outcome could result in David establishing himself in a strong position of authority (The Emperor), and by leading by example he could teach others how to advance themselves both materially and spiritually (The Pope).

Step Six: *Reading the vertical lines*
The seven vertical lines, each in a group of three cards, bring David's issue into sharp focus.

Line One: Inherent Characteristics (Talents and gifts) King of Money, Ace of Clubs, Three of Swords
> David has a natural gift for creating material wealth, security and comforts. He has an abundance of energy and imaginative ideas and uses his innate cleverness well.

Line Two: Insight (Self-awareness and separation) Ten of Clubs, Four of Swords, Death
> David is aware of his restlessness and the urge to consolidate his talents for some as yet unidentified purpose. Unrealized aspirations need a more structured approach to his thinking and deliberations that could result in the transformation he desires.

Line Three: Intuition (Reconciliation and the realm of the senses) Ace of Cups, Five of Cups, Ten of Swords
> Intuition, sensuality, sensuousness have to be the guiding and dominant force in his life. He may now be thinking about doing something with a more altruistic motive.

Line Four: Instinct (Self-discipline, rationality and leadership)
Seven of Cups, The Lover, Four of Cups

David knows that the imminent cyclical changes in his life will demand that he takes a step in a new direction.

Line Five: Introspection (Spiritual awareness, values and order)
Queen of Cups, The Chariot, Two of Swords

The Queen tells us David has a natural gift to bring peace, love and tranquillity into his life and the lives of those around him. He is caught in two minds about embarking on any new venture that may put at risk his current way of life and lifestyle.

Line Six: Indecision (Making choices and/or marriage of ideas or relationships) Eight of Clubs, Three of Money, The Emperor

The right choices made now could result in David revitalizing his energies in a way that could bring him renewed pleasures and satisfaction on both the material and spiritual planes. In turn, this could change his current restlessness to give way to a sense of order and purpose that would reap benefits to himself and others within his sphere of influence.

Line Seven: Independence (Outcome of a journey into the unknown; courage to let go of the reins) Knight of Money, Two of Clubs, The Pope

It may be in David's mind to use his abilities to generate wealth in order to revitalize his energies and follow a new path that will bring greater inner satisfaction to himself and lead the way for the benefit of others.

Step Seven: *Concluding the reading*

After the reading, David told me he was a happily married man with grown up children who enjoyed a comfortable life. He was a 'self-made man' who, over the years, had been involved in various businesses – some were more successful than others – but overall, his enterprises had provided him and his family with a substantial house in England, a villa abroad, a good income and independence.

He said the reading had helped him to bring into focus and acknowledge a restlessness in what he was doing with his life. At the back of his mind he was aware that he wanted a change in direction and the reading had given him a clearer picture about what he might do, and where he could use his business experience and skills to satisfy his desire to do something more than just making money and earning a living.

Example Reading Two: Zoe

This reading was for a young woman in her mid-twenties who will be referred to as Zoe. She is vivacious, handsome, sensuous and outgoing. She was dressed in a somewhat flamboyant and individualistically stylish manner and appeared to have a zest for life but was not entirely at ease with herself. (As usual, her 'issue' was not discussed before the reading.) Below is the layout of her spread:

Step One: *The Significator*
In this reading the Significator card in the centre space number 11 is the Three of Cups. This card suggests Zoe's issues concern her emotional life and how to achieve a resolution to reach fulfilment in mind, body and spirit. The appearance of the Major Arcana cards Justice, The Hermit, and The Wheel of Fortune, and the Nine and Ten of Cups and Swords indicates Zoe needs to allow herself a period for contemplation and recapitulation on what has been happening to her before rushing into anything new.

Step Two: *Reviewing the number of Major Arcana cards in the spread.*
As noted before, on average, there will be six or seven in any one spread due to the ratio of one Major card for seven Minor cards in the pack.

There are five Major cards in the spread:

IV The Emperor	defining one's boundaries
VII Justice	striving for balance
VIIII The Hermit	making time for contemplation
X The Wheel of Fortune	accepting inevitable changes
XX The World	nourishment and fulfilment

Step Three: *Reviewing the predominance of any one suit and any cards bearing the same numbers*

2, 5, 6, 8, 9, 10 and King of Swords	Zoe's thoughts about her current personal relationships, career and the general direction her life is taking have been constantly on her mind.
2, 3, 9 and 10 of Cups	The similarity of numbers with the suit of Swords suggests her uppermost concern is about emotional situations.
Ace, 5 and King of Clubs	Zoe has strong energy levels and is gifted with imaginative creativity.
7 and King of Money	There may be changes in her circumstances.

The predominance of Swords and Cups suggest that intellectual pursuits and charged emotional experiences – the stuff of poets and writers – have been uppermost in her mind. The Two of Swords and Two of Cups indicate that whatever are her concerns she cannot make up her mind; she is subject to self-doubt and is feeling unsettled. The three number nines – Nine of Swords, Nine of Cups and The Hermit – are demanding time for reflection to review the current situation in her career or relationships. The three number tens – Ten of Swords, Ten of Cups and The Wheel of Fortune, suggest that taking time out for a while will allow her energy and ideas to evolve to a new level.

FIGURE 27: ZOE'S SPREAD

Line 1 **1** TEN OF CUPS   **2** EIGHT OF SWORDS **3** THE WORLD

Line 2 **8** JUSTICE   **9** KING OF CLUBS   **10** TWO OF CUPS

Line 3 **15** SEVEN OF MONEY **16** THE HERMIT   **17** TWO OF SWORD

4 THE EMPEROR   **5** SIX OF SWORDS   **6** NINE OF CUPS   **7** FIVE OF SWORDS

11 THREE OF CUPS   **12** NINE OF SWORDS   **13** KING OF SWORDS   **14** FIVE OF CLUBS

18 ACE OF CLUBS   **19** TEN OF SWORDS   **20** KNAVE OF MONEY   **21** WHEEL OF FORTUNE

Step Four: *Reviewing the eight cards surrounding the Significator*

Line one	place numbers 4, 11, 18
Line two	place numbers 10, 11, 12
Line three	place numbers 3, 11, 19
Line four	place numbers 5, 11, 17

This will give a broad synopsis of Zoe's main issue and the direction the reading will take.

Line One: The Ace of Clubs signals Zoe's imaginative gifts and talents. To manifest her creative energies in the outer world she needs to define boundaries and exercise discipline (The Emperor) to achieve the emotional fulfilment to be resolved by the Three of Cups.

Line Two: The current emotional conflict (Two of Cups) may be overcome if Zoe takes time out for non-judgemental, detached introspection to review the things that have worked and not worked so far in her life (Nine of Swords).

Line Three: The Ten of Swords is about how to take her thoughts, ideas and aspirations onto another plane where she will find the satisfaction and pleasure that will embrace her emotional needs (The World).

Line Four: The Two of Swords suggest that Zoe is caught in two minds about which direction to take, but whatever she decides she would like others to benefit as well as herself.

Step Five: *Reading the horizontal lines*
The top line (place numbers 1 to 7) tells us where Zoe is now, in the material world.

The middle line (place numbers 8 to 14) tells us something about what matters / issues are currently occupying her thoughts.

The bottom line (place numbers 15 to 21) tells us what may be at the back of her mind, her unexpressed ideas and perhaps where she would like to be heading.

The Top Line: Here is a young woman with a big heart who does not bear grudges (Ten of Cups and Eight of Swords); she is constantly trying out new ideas and finding ways to express her gift to dance with life and for the pleasure of others (The Emperor and The World). New thought patterns may be emerging (Six of Swords) but, as the direction is not clear at the moment, Zoe needs time to count her own blessings and to recharge her energies before embarking on new enterprises (Nine of Cups and Five of Swords).

The Middle Line: Zoe is beginning to address how to bring balance, order and harmony into her life (Justice and Three of Cups) which might lead to her harnessing the Feminine and Masculine Principles (Kings of Clubs and Swords) to develop and channel her natural high energy levels. This could also resolve the present dichotomy (Two of Cups) in her emotional issues.

The Bottom Line: Zoe's current material and financial circumstances may be on the verge of changing (Seven of Money) and leading her to distance herself from personal relationship involvements and career activities (The Hermit), bringing about a period of time to sort out the present confusion (Two of Swords). This could allow her natural talent, her inspiration, creative ideas and aspirations to evolve to a more rewarding level. The Knave of Money indicates that Zoe is already preparing the foundations but she needs to keep 'grounded' with an inner resolve and self-awareness and be open to let Fate (The Wheel of Fortune) take a hand.

Step Six: *Reading the vertical lines*

This final reading of the group of three cards in each of the seven vertical lines brings Zoe's issue into sharp focus.

> **Line One: Inherent Characteristics** (Talents and gifts) Ten of Cups, Justice, Seven of Money
>
> The Ten of Cups tells us Zoe has a heightened sense of emotional output and charged experiences that she can bring into focus to create balance and harmony in her life, which will help her deal with the pattern of changes in her material/financial circumstances.

> **Line Two: Insight** (Self-awareness and separation) Eight of Swords, King of Clubs, The Hermit
>
> Zoe's current mode of thinking about how to harness her creative energies might be best served by temporarily withdrawing to receive a guiding hand from her own intuition. Meditation and solitude could help her to discover more of herself and her core values.

> **Line Three: Intuition** (Reconciliation and the realm of the senses) The World, Two of Cups, Two of Swords
>
> Outwardly, Zoe has an abundant zest for life and living; she can dance with joy and has a gift for creating pleasure, but inwardly there are self-doubts about her relationships, her past emotional experiences and whether, at the present time, she is able or willing to take decisive action. In other words, she may not always trust her intuition which can result in her falling into a state of limbo.

> **Line Four: Instinct** (Self-discipline, rationality and leadership) The Emperor, Three of Cups, Ace of Clubs
>
> Zoe needs to firmly establish boundaries in her personal life and career. The Emperor also reminds Zoe to trust her instincts, be assertive, be true to herself and accept responsibility in all her

undertakings. Such forthright action and attitude might bring about the emotional fulfilment and the outlet for the expression of her many talents and potentialities.

It should be noted here that in this spread The Emperor occupies the same space as it does in the 21-card spread of the Major Arcana (see Figure 23).

Line Five: Introspection (Spiritual awareness, values and order)
Six of Swords, Nine of Swords, Ten of Swords
Zoe's thought patterns are demanding her to devote quality time to review her current circumstances so that her concepts are able to evolve and develop before rushing into processes.

Line 6: Indecision (Making choices and/or marriage of ideas or relationships)
9 of Cups, King of Swords, Knave of Money
Again, important decisions might best be postponed for the time being until Zoe feels her emotional energies have been replenished and recharged before tackling the challenges ahead and possible changes in lifestyle.

Line Seven: Independence (Outcome of a journey into the unknown; courage to let go of the reins) Five of Swords, Five of Clubs, The Wheel of Fortune
The Five of Swords and Clubs suggest that her work and creativity may be most rewarding if directed towards being beneficial to others as well as herself. This holistic, humanitarian approach may be a way forward to resolve her current work, relationships and material circumstances.

Step Seven: *Concluding the reading*
After the reading, Zoe said she had recently broken up with a long-time lover. Her career activities were completely involved in the world of showbusiness and entertainment. She is a professional dancer and teacher; she directs and acts in the theatre, hopes to be a

full-time jazz singer and plays several musical instruments.

Here is a young woman who is almost a victim of her own multi-talented abilities, who finds it difficult to focus on any one specific choice which results in frustration and fragmentation of her energies. She confirmed she needed to set and consolidate her boundaries and to allow herself the 'luxury' of time and space.

8

THE TAROT AS A CODE FOR LIVING

There exists a universal wisdom embracing a knowledge of Man and the Universe. For those prepared by their own efforts to penetrate beyond the outer veil of appearances to the reality of knowledge, this wisdom can be perceived. The path to knowing has ever been open to those who are determined to set their feet on the ladder towards illumination.[1]

This book has focused on using the powerful archetypal images of the Tarot as a means to gain insights into our human nature which can guide us along the path to self-understanding and awareness. I believe the fundamental principles and wisdom expressed in the 21 Major Arcana cards can also provide us with a positive code of conduct – a maxim of principles, if you will – to live by on a day-to-day basis, as illustrated in the following examples.

'A Personal Code for Living' sets out a suggested way of living our private lives. Furthermore, such a code could be modified as a charter to improve the conduct of the two most significant influences that impinge on our lives, namely the powers of business/economics and politics. Of course, the Tarot makes us aware that before we can influence and change the negative external forces in the world about us, we must first begin to review our own thought processes, actions and reactions: we have to deal with our own *shadow* before crusading to change others. A meditation devoted to each card can reveal and awaken deep insights into our own true Self that penetrate beyond the ego and self-illusion.

'A Charter for Business' is an example of a code for those who are either employers or employees, while 'A Charter for Politicians' is an example of a code for those in national or local politics. Essentially, the economics of business are concerned with making material gains that are not always in the best interests of people, ecology and the planet. It could also be said that, despite politicians' usual protests that their motives are purely altruistic, they set themselves up to become local, national or international politicians because they have a deep-seated belief that only *they* know best how we should live our lives. In the 21st century, the world is a global village and whether we are a Western city dweller or an Amazonian Indian living in the depths of the jungle, our lives and the way we live will be affected, to a greater or lesser extent, by these all-pervading external forces.

A PERSONAL CODE FOR LIVING

1 To act with integrity and use my gifts and talents for the highest good (The Magician).
2 To acknowledge the principle of 'As above, so below' – the material world is complemented by an invisible realm (The High Priestess).
3 To be guided by intuition and to respect and care for others and the natural world (The Empress).
4 To encourage human endeavour, protect personal freedoms and balance the head with the heart (The Emperor).
5 To honour and live by moral principles (The Pope).
6 To encourage creativity and follow the dictates of conscience (The Lover).

7 To be courageous with fortitude (The Chariot).

8 To strive for justice and fair dealings (Justice).

9 To allow due time for contemplation and introspection (The Hermit).

10 To be adaptable to change, accept personal responsibility for one's actions and avoid blaming others for misfortunes that befall me (The Wheel of Fortune).

11 To strive for self-awareness and self-understanding (Force).

12 To balance spontaneous action with time needed for conceptual thought (The Hanged Man).

13 To accept that changes are inevitable (Death).

14 To acknowledge and express the eternal life force of the human spirit (Temperance).

15 To guard against self-doubt and beware the manipulation of others (The Devil).

16 To acknowledge the gifts/talents of others and avoid self-aggrandizement (The Tower of Destruction).

17 To tread lightly over the Earth and protect, replenish and sustain natural resources (The Star).

18 To avoid self-deception and illusion (The Moon).

19 To be transparent, truthful and exercise independence of spirit and conscience (The Sun).

20 To become that which you already are (Judgement).

21 To be positive, live life to the full and for the benefit of others and contribute to the creation of a healthy and better World (The World).

0 To treat mistakes and failings as well as triumphs as a necessary part of the process of travelling from naivety to maturity and becoming 'a man/woman of knowledge': wisdom is determined by how that knowledge is used (The Fool).

A CHARTER FOR BUSINESS

Imagine the consequences if every chief executive, member of the
board of directors and managers of any organization had to swear on
oath to uphold the principles of this charter.

1 I will acknowledge the gifts and abilities of others to
   contribute to our enterprise (The Magician).

2 I accept there is an occult (hidden) dimension that is
   complemented with the material world (The High
   Priestess).

3 I will allow my intuition to guide me in making
   decisions that will best nurture and care for people and
   the natural world (The Empress).

4 I will encourage human endeavour and balance rationality with the need to act for the highest good (The
   Emperor).

5 I will respect social values, moral principles and act
   according to conscience (The Pope).

6 I will encourage creativity and base choices on long-term
   rather than short-term, expedient benefits (The Lover).

7 I do have the courage to follow my intuition and instinct
   and will allow free rein to others (The Chariot).

8 I will respect law and order and act fairly in all my
   dealings (Justice).

9 I will allow due time for given tasks and concept development (The Hermit).

10 I will adapt to changing circumstances and events and
    avoid laying blame on others (The Wheel of Fortune).

11 I will strive for self-knowledge (Force).

12 Spontaneous ideas and innovations will be given due
    time to evolve (The Hanged Man).

13 I accept the inevitability of change (Death).

14 I respect the life force of the human spirit (Temperance).

15 I will avoid manipulating others (Devil).

16 I will acknowledge the contributions made by others
    (The Tower of Destruction).

17 Sustainability, protection of natural resources and
    ecology will be included on all business agendas and
    given due consideration (The Star).

18 I will not tolerate deception and creating illusions
    (The Moon).

19 All dealings will be transparent (The Sun).

20 I am and will be receptive to new ideas and suggestions
    (Judgement).

21 The core aim of the business will be to contribute to
    sustainability and making the world a better place
    (The World).

0   I accept I will make mistakes and will take immediate
    corrective action (The Fool).

A CHARTER FOR POLITICIANS

Imagine the consequences if every politician had to swear an oath to
uphold these principles:

1 My policies will be dedicated to enhance and enrich our
   lives and to make the World a better, safer place
   (The Magician).

2 I accept there is more to life than materiality and
   material gain (The High Priestess).

3 I will follow my intuition and only support policies
   which protect and nurture people and the Planet
   (The Empress).

4 I will encourage human endeavour and protect personal
   freedoms (The Emperor).

5 I will honour social and traditional values and perennial
   wisdom, and uphold moral principles (The Pope).

6 I will only follow the dictates of my conscience (The Lover).

7   I will act with courage and fortitude (The Chariot).

8   I will strive for justice and equitable law and order (Justice).

9   My support for any policy will be determined by the dictates of my personal integrity rather than political allegiances or expediencies (The Hermit).

10 I will accept responsibility for all my actions without retribution or laying blame on others (The Wheel of Fortune).

11 I will constantly review my pride, prejudices and any ulterior motives (Force).

12 I will not support any ill-considered or poorly drafted legislation (The Hanged Man).

13 I accept the need to exercise flexibility in response to inevitable changes that will occur (Death).

14 I acknowledge that my personal attitude of mind can/will influence whether an issue has either a positive or negative outcome (Temperance).

15 I will not engage in unscrupulous manipulation of information and events (The Devil).

16 I will acknowledge the contributions others may make and not indulge in self-aggrandizement (The Tower of Destruction).

17 Sustainability, the protection of nature and replenishment of natural resources will be the paramount factors determining my support for any policy or proposal (The Star).

18 I will guard against any form of self-deception or illusion (The Moon).

19 I will be truthful and exercise my independence of spirit and conscience (The Sun).

20 I will welcome and be receptive to the emergence of new ideas and thinking (Judgement).

21 I will strive to make the world a better, healthier, safer and more enjoyable place for the benefit of all (The World).

0   I will strive to learn by my mistakes and use that knowledge as wisely as possible (The Fool).

Whilst it may be optimistic to believe there would be many business people and politicians willing to swear to abide by these principles, as individuals we have the free will to sign up to live according to our own personal code of conduct based on the tenets of the Tarot. To live by such a code could create a paradigm shift where materiality and spirituality are more in balance in the world of business and also bring about a change in politicians to overcome their underlying thirst for the power that demands party allegiances, short-term expediencies and often a conflict of conscience.

9

CONCLUSION

And the end of all our exploring
Will be to arrive where we started,
And to know the place for the first time.[1]

W hen we open our eyes for the first time, we are
in a state of bliss and at one with the World. All
too soon, we have to come to terms with
survival, disease, crime, poverty and riches,
personal relationships, business, politics, life and death. How these
concepts and conditions control our attitudes to personal responsibilities, towards other people, to society in general, to the planet Earth
and to the invisible Universe depends on how we relate to ourselves.
There will always be challenges that balance our natural instincts for
survival and the desire for gratification with the need to have a deeper
understanding of 'Who am I?', 'Why am I here?' and 'What is my
destiny?' The Tarot tells us that to answer these questions each one of
us must undertake a journey into the unknown psychospiritual realms
of the unconscious mind. This demands courage, fortitude and
someone or something to guide us on our way.

Throughout the history of humankind, every culture has recognized the need for both children and adults to be initiated in terms of
their self-development and awareness of the invisible realms to enable
them to take a responsible part in society. The ancient mystery schools
evolved to provide initiates with 'a map and compass' to explore the
phenomena of nature and the physical world as well as their own
human nature and the inner worlds of the psyche and spirit. Vestiges
of the mystery school teachings still exist covertly in the West.

Other forms of initiation are practised by the so-called 'primitive' tribes that still exist on every continent. For example, in the Australian bush a mother of a young boy must say 'goodbye' to her son as he leaves her side to go with the elders of the tribe into the bush. The initiation lasts a few days. First, he is hand-fed and treated as if he is still a baby in arms. Later, alone in the darkness, he believes the sound of the men whirling their whining bull-roarers is actually a frenzied monster. The terrified young neophyte is convinced he is about to be devoured by this hideous creature. Ritually, this near-death experience is essential for him to *die* as a child before he can be *reborn* as a man. His experience and survival of the ordeal that transforms his status from neophyte to initiate prepares him to receive the secret teachings of the tribe. When he is led back to the village his new status as a mature, initiated member of the society is acknowledged and confirmed when he is 'introduced' to his mother as if he were a stranger. As a young initiate, the first step he takes on his *heroic journey* has been to sever the psychological umbilical cord from his mother. These rites of passage – going into the wilderness, suffering death, resurrection and revelation – follow a recognizable and universal pattern throughout the World.

In his book, *Rites and Symbols of Initiation,* Mercia Eliade says, 'Every man wants to experience certain perilous situations, to confront exceptional ordeals to make his way into the other World – and he experiences all this on the level of his imaginative life by hearing and reading fairy tales.'[2]

In other words, it is in our nature to want to experience some form of a rite of passage such as that symbolically expressed in the Tarot. Sadly, today, the classical myths and fairy tales have become expurgated, dumbed-down 'adaptations' served up by the cinema and TV as entertainment for children. In our intellectually-based, materialistic society there is an absence of sacred practices that leaves a gaping, unhealed wound in the collective unconsciousness of the Western World, which leads to teenage boys and girls finding their own, often highly dangerous, *exceptional ordeals*. Why do we ignore and suppress the wisdom of our 'men/women of knowledge'? Why have we lost our sense of the divinity of the soul and the Cosmos?

Our Western *civilization* tends to ignore many of the fundamental elements of human nature. We no longer have any ritualized form of initiation that was so well understood and acknowledged by ancient traditions. Today, there is no respect for the wise men and women and there are thousands of households where the father is absent, leaving the children – especially the boys – to grow up knowing only their mother. The boys are desperate to break away – to cut the umbilical cord – to *experience certain perilous situations and ordeals* and many can only turn to crime and violence on the streets to test their courage and endurance. Government policies, political correctness and an overzealous Health and Safety Executive have even barred the opportunities for competitive sports in our schools!

The whole of society will increasingly suffer social dysfunctions whilst we, the elders of our respective 'tribes' – the parents, politicians, teachers and lawyers – persist in continuing this perverse disservice towards our young people. How can we bring about the necessary fundamental changes to improve the quality of life for us all?

A more readily available source today in the 21st century is the Tarot cards: these can also effectively guide us – the adult neophytes – along a path of initiation into the mysteries of Nature. The Tarot offers an enlightened guide to personal integrity and responsibility for all one's actions and thoughts. On the pathway we come face to face with our illusions, experience intuitive, instinctive insights and discover the occult world where, ultimately, we will find our true Selves. This is the mythical journey that leads to fulfilment. In other words, The Fool within us all is transformed from naïve foolishness into becoming the 'man/woman of wisdom and knowledge'.

As a serious Querant, each one of us needs to sense at which point or milestone we are now standing on our journey before we can understand what to do to take the next step forward. For just a minute or two, using intuitive introspection, carefully look at each of the Major cards in the layout in figure 23. Then close your eyes and hold the images in a visual meditation: you may find that you are drawn to one particular card which will most likely indicate the milestone marker where you are currently standing and what needs to be your next step to make progress along the path.

At the end of the Tarot's journey we will have healed ourselves, discharged sorrow, become integrated with the *Anima Mundi* (the World Soul) and fulfilled our innate greatness, and then – finally – we realize that we have to begin yet again to summon up our strength to continue the climb higher up the infinite spiral of self-knowledge.

ENDNOTES

Introduction
1 Geahart, Sally, and Rennie, Susan, *A Feminist Tarot*, p xii

1 Tarot Through The Ages
1 Walker, Barbara G, *Woman's Encyclopaedia of Myths and Secrets*, p 977
2 Hall, Manly P, *The Secret Teachings of All Ages*, pcxxix
3 Walker, Barbara G, *The Secrets of the Tarot*, p 13
4 Beaulieu and Baylé, *Le Costume en Bourgogne*, plates i–xi
5 Brummel, Beau, *Male and Female Costume*, p 67
6 Blakely, JD, *The Mystical Tower of the Tarot*, p 16, citing Paul Marteau, *Le Tarot de Marseille*, Paris Arts et Métiers Graphiques, 1949
7 Hawking, Stephen, *A Brief History of Time*, p 166

2 The Mythical Journey of the Hero/Heroine
1 Campbell, Joseph, *The Hero with a Thousand Faces*, p 31
2 Apuleius, Lucius, *The Golden Ass*, pp 67–99
3 Heline, Corinne, *The Bible and the Tarot*, p 129
4 Shakespeare, William, *Hamlet*, Act III, Scene i
5 Dahlke, R and Dethlefsen, T, *The Healing Power of Illness*, pp 36, 39, 40
6 Castaneda, Carlos, *The Teachings of Don Juan*, p 84
7 Castaneda, Carlos, *The Teachings of Don Juan*, p 87

3 The Language of the Tarot
1 Raine, Kathleen, *Yeats the Initiate*, p 246
2 Baldock, John, *The Alternative Gospel*, p 72
3 Baldock, John, *The Elements of Christian Symbolism*, pp 1–2
4 Hall, Manly P, *The Secret Teachings of All Ages*, p xx
5 Baldock, John, unpublished extract from a draft of
   The Alternative Gospel
6 Hall, Manly P, *The Secret Teachings of All Ages*, p cxx

7 Line, Julia, *The Numerology Workbook*, p 11
8 Haich, Elisabeth, *Wisdom of the Tarot*, p 81
9 Cirlot, JE, *A Dictionary of Symbols*, p 234
10 *Readers' Digest Universal Dictionary*
11 *The Shorter Oxford English Dictionary*

4 Decoding the Major Arcana

1 Lecture by Robert Bly, *c*.1990
2 Walker, Barbara G, *Woman's Dictionary of Symbols and Sacred Objects*, pp 9, 10
3 Machiavelli, *The Prince*, chapter xxv, page 84

6 Encoding The Tarot's Journey

1 Proust, Marcel, *Remembrance of Times Past*, volume 7
2 Nichols, Sallie, *Jung and Tarot: An Archetypal Journey* (from the Introduction by Laurens van der Post), p xiv
3 Nichols, Sallie, *Jung and Tarot: An Archetypal Journey* (from the Introduction by Laurens van der Post), p xv

7 Reading A Spread

1 *The Sunday Telegraph*, 14 April 1991

8 The Tarot as a Code for Living

1 Mills, Joy, *Research Into Lost Knowledge Organization*, Number 64, p 15

9 Conclusion

1 Eliot, TS, *Little Gidding*, from *Four Quartets*, p 197
2 Eliade, Mercia, *Rites and Symbols of Initiation*, p 126

BIBLIOGRAPHY

Apuleius, Lucius, *The Golden Ass*, translated by Robert Graves, Penguin, London, 1950

Baldock, John, *The Alternative Gospel*, Element Books, Shaftesbury, 1997

Baldock, John, *The Elements of Christian Symbolism*, Element Books, Shaftesbury, 1990

Beaulieu and Baylé, *Le Costume en Bourgogne*, Presses Universitaires de France, 1956

Blakely, JD, *The Mystical Tower of the Tarot*, Robinson & Watkins Books Ltd, London, 1974

Brummel, Beau, *Male and Female Costume*, Doubleday, Deran and Co. Inc., New York

Campbell, Joseph, *The Hero with a Thousand Faces*, Grafton Books, London, 1988

Castaneda, Carlos, *The Teachings of Don Juan*, Penguin Books, Harmondsworth, 1970

Cirlot, JE, *A Dictionary of Symbols*, Routledge & Keegan Paul, London, 1983

Dahlke, R, and Dethlefsen, T, *The Healing Power of Illness*, Element Books, Shaftesbury, 1992

Eliade, Mercia, *Rites and Symbols of Initiation*, Harper and Row, New York, 1975

Eliot, TS, *The Four Quartets*, Faber and Faber, London, 2004

Geahart, Sally, and Rennie, Susan, *A Feminist Tarot*, Alyson Publishers Inc, Boston, 1981

Haich, Elisabeth, *Wisdom of the Tarot*, Allen and Unwin, London, 1985

Hall, Manly P, *The Secret Teachings of All Ages*, The Philosophical Research Society, Inc, CA, 1997

Hawking, Stephen, *A Brief History of Time*, Bantam Press, London, 1988

Heline, Corinne, *The Bible and the Tarot*, New Age Press Inc, CA, 1984

Line, Julia, *The Numerology Workbook*, The Aquarian Press, Wellingborough, 1985

Machiavelli, Niccolo, *The Prince*, translated by NH Thomson, PF
    Collier and Son, 1910

Nichols, Sallie, *Jung and Tarot: An Archetypal Journey* (Introduction by
    Laurens van der Post), S Weiser Inc, Maine, 1980

Proust, Marcel, *Remembrance of Things Past*, translated by CK Scott
    Moncrieff and Terence Kilmartin, Penguin Books Ltd, London,
    1986

Raine, Kathleen, *Yeats the Initiate*, Dolmen Press, Ireland, 1986

Walker, Barbara G, *The Secrets of the Tarot*, Harper and Row, New
    York, 1984

Walker, Barbara G, *Woman's Dictionary of Symbols and Sacred Objects*,
    Harper and Row, San Francisco, 1988

Walker, Barbara G, *Woman's Encyclopaedia of Myths and Secrets*,
    Harper and Row, San Francisco, 1983

INDEX